STRATEGIC LEADERSHIP

HOW TO DEVELOP OWNERSHIP AND BUILD FUTURE LEADERS

JAMIE ANNE GUSTAFSON, PHD

ISBNs:

eBook: 979-8-9945750-0-0

Paperback: 979-8-9945750-1-7

Book Cover: The Creative 5280

Senior Editor and Interior Design: Andrea Lard, The Creative 5280

Editor: Kay Lard, The Creative 5280

CONTENTS

A NOTE OF GRATITUDE

Before we dive into the pages ahead, I want to take a moment to express my heartfelt thanks to the people who have been my guiding lights.

To my husband, thank you for teaching me to embrace the joy and love of the process itself, rather than focusing solely on the outcomes. Your wisdom has been a gift that has shaped not only this book but so much of my life.

To my friends, the heartbeat of my thoughts, your support has been my constant source of strength. A special thank you to Kaitlyn, Jessica, Vanessa, and Alex—your encouragement, feedback, and belief in me have been instrumental in bringing this book and my fierceness to life.

To my parents, you built the foundation of who I am today. You gave me opposite but equally vital traits that have become the pillars of my daily success. Your love and guidance are woven into every word of this book.

And to my son, Dylan, thank you for teaching me the value of truly seeing people—not just through my own lens, but through theirs. You remind me every day of the beauty in connection and understanding.

Thank you for being part of my journey.

PREFACE

Leadership is not a title, a position, or a destination; it's a journey. It's a process of growth, resilience, and intentionality that transforms individuals and organizations alike. This book is born from my own journey, one shaped by challenges, triumphs, and a relentless commitment to service, strategic thinking, and leadership development.

From becoming a mother as a teenager to serving my country through military deployment, to guiding businesses through succession plans, and employees through ownership journeys, I've learned that leadership is forged in the crucible of experience.

It's about showing up prepared, resilient, and rooted in purpose. These lessons have guided me through community initiatives, academic pursuits, and the development of small businesses, each chapter deepening my understanding of what it means to lead with intention.

As a consultant, I've had the privilege of working with organizations to bridge the gap between vision and execution. My focus on succession planning has allowed me to help businesses prepare for the future by cultivating leadership at every level. I've guided many individuals and teams through the Five Stages of Ownership, a framework I developed to transform contributors into intentional leaders. I believe this journey is the key to driving innovation, fostering connection, and creating a culture where leadership thrives.

In addition to my consulting work, I've had the honor of serving as a professor, sharing my passion for leadership and strategic management with the next generation of leaders. My academic journey, culminating in a PhD in Strategic Management, has provided me with the tools to combine real-world experience with research-based insights. This unique perspective has shaped the frameworks and strategies you'll find in this book.

At its core, this book is about a simple but profound truth—leadership is either designed or accidental. Too often, organizations rely on attrition or immediate need to fill leadership roles, leaving potential untapped and teams unprepared. This book is my response to that gap, a guide to fostering ownership, cultivating strategic thinking, and creating a culture where leadership emerges at every level. It introduces practical tools and frameworks, such as the 5-Stage Ownership Journey, to help you intentionally develop leaders and design conditions for long-term success.

Reading this book is just the beginning. Leadership development doesn't stop with understanding; it requires action. I invite you to stop promoting by accident and start developing leaders. The next step is execution, and I've designed a course to help you put these principles into practice. Together, we'll take the insights from this book and turn them into actionable strategies that will transform your organization and the leaders within it.

The insights you'll find here are not just theoretical. They are drawn from my experiences as a consultant, professor, and leader, as well as from the stories of individuals and organizations that have embarked on the journey of leadership formation. I hope that this book will provide you with the tools, confidence, and language to contribute meaningfully, lead effectively, and build a foundation for sustainable growth.

Leadership is a shared journey, and I'm honored to walk this path with you. Together, we can create a future in which leadership is not merely a role but a way of being, one that inspires, empowers, and transforms.

Welcome to the journey.

—Jamie Anne Gustafson, PhD

INTRODUCTION
BUILDING A STRATEGIC
FOUNDATION FOR LEADERSHIP

Organizations do not struggle with leadership because their people are incapable, unmotivated, or unintelligent. They struggle because the process that turns employees into leaders is fundamentally broken.

Every day, we see the same pattern play out. Capable, committed individuals are promoted to leadership roles based on tenure, urgency, or technical skill. Yet, they are rarely taught how to think critically, make strategic decisions, or take ownership beyond their individual responsibilities. Leadership is often assigned through attrition or immediate need rather than intentionally developed. We assign leadership, but we do not form leaders.

The result is a familiar cycle that frustrates everyone involved—high-performing employees become overwhelmed managers, teams lose clarity, and organizational progress stalls. This doesn't happen because of a lack of effort. It occurs due to a lack of formation. High-potential talent observes this struggle, loses faith and trust in the system, and disengages.

This book exists to address that gap. The system is broken, and this book is here to fix it.

As a business owner, executive, manager, or organizational stakeholder, including those seeking to chart their own trajectory within an organization, you already understand that your company's greatest asset is its people. The question isn't whether your people are capable. The real question is: **How do you help them become leaders before you give them the title?**

This book is designed to be that bridge between potential and performance. It is an intentional investment in ownership, strategic thinking, and participative leadership from the start.

It challenges all stakeholders to view the business as a connected system, see the bigger picture, and recognize their specific role in shaping outcomes. True leadership does not begin with authority; it begins with how people think, decide, and engage long before a promotion is ever considered.

At the core of this transformation is strategic awareness—not only through performing a Strength-First SWOT analysis, but by actively developing an implementation plan that emphasizes strengths, counters weaknesses, and seizes opportunities. When employees understand an organization's Strengths, Weaknesses, Opportunities, and Threats (SWOT), and can map a path for action, their perspective shifts. They move from task completion to contextual decision-making. They begin to understand not just *what* they are doing, but *why* it matters.

This approach changes behavior. An employee who understands a company's strengths can help maximize them in daily work. Someone who spots a weakness can develop real solutions rather than encounter the same roadblocks. When teams are prepared to jump on opportunities and actively defend against threats, proactive thinking and shared responsibility for the organization's future take hold.

Autonomy and confidence are built not through instruction alone, but through understanding. Innovation, in this sense, is not accidental; it is cultivated. Some of the most valuable ideas in any organization come from those closest to the work. When people are given strategic context and permission to think critically, they become an internal engine for innovation. Their ideas evolve from disconnected suggestions into informed initiatives rooted in the business landscape.

When those insights are invited, heard, and acted upon, something powerful happens—ownership takes hold.

Ownership is often mistaken for control, but it is actually about connection. This book is written for those who recognize a hard truth: leadership does not fail because people lack talent or commitment; it fails because development is left to chance.

For the Leader and Stakeholder:

This book offers you a new lens for leadership formation. It provides a shared language and frameworks to identify leadership potential early, cultivate strategic thinking before promotion, and design conditions that enable strategic thinking capacity to grow over time. Rather than reacting to leadership gaps as they arise, this book helps you prevent them by intentionally developing yourself and others.

For the Employee:

If you want to contribute more meaningfully, this book gives you context, confidence, and language. It helps you understand how organizations work as systems, how decisions are made, and how ownership manifests before a title ever changes. You will see how strategic thinking, initiative, and participation build credibility and influence, even without formal authority. Most importantly, you will recognize that leadership is not something you wait to be given. It is something you practice.

The themes in this book, decision-making, confidence, and self-empowerment, are deeply personal to me. My own journey has been shaped by moments of uncertainty, responsibility, and growth long before I ever held formal authority. I became a mother as a teenager, served on military deployment, led community initiatives, and earned my doctorate through persistence and grit. Each chapter of my life reinforced the same lesson—real impact comes from clear thinking, strategic decision-making, and the ability to turn challenge into opportunity.

These experiences inform the foundation of this book, but the focus is not my story. It is the process behind it. One concept that runs throughout these pages is the idea of "taking up space."

Taking up space is not about dominance or ego; it is about owning your role, your decisions, and your contributions. When people are empowered to decide, create, and contribute, they develop confidence not because they are told to, but because they have practiced it.

Leaders strengthen organizations by creating environments where decision-making is encouraged, feedback is valued, and struggle is calibrated, not eliminated. Giving people room to think and choose builds trust, loyalty, and innovation. These are not abstract ideals—they are conditions that can be intentionally designed.

Leadership does not emerge fully formed. It develops gradually, through repeated exposure to responsibility, decision-making, and ownership. Over time, I began to see a clear pattern in how people grow into leadership roles and, just as importantly, where that growth breaks down when development is left to chance.

That pattern became the foundation for what I call the **5-Stage Ownership Journey**.

This journey is a developmental roadmap that reflects how ownership and leadership actually form inside organizations. It is not a performance rating system, a checklist, or a promotion ladder. Instead, it is a way to recognize growth as it happens, to understand how awareness becomes alignment, how insight turns into action, and how initiative evolves into true ownership.

As you move through this book, each chapter will support one or more stages of this journey. You will not find step-by-step training modules here. Instead, you will find frameworks, stories, and mental models that help leaders recognize ownership, cultivate it early, and build systems that support leadership development well before promotion.

Whether you are guiding others or growing yourself, the goal is the same: strategic thinking, better decisions, and organizations that deliberately develop leaders rather than by accident.

When organizations intentionally develop ownership, they create teams that are resilient, adaptive, and invested. Employees stop working *for* the company and begin working *with* it. Strategic thinking is distributed across the system rather than relying on a few individuals at the top.

Handing this book to an employee sends a clear message: *Your voice matters here. We trust you to think critically. We want you involved in building what comes next.*

This is not traditional onboarding. It is leadership formation. Let's begin.

PART ONE
WHY LEADERSHIP
FORMATION FAILS

1

THE ACCIDENTAL
LEADER PROBLEM

"The accidental leader survives the moment—the strategic leader shapes the future. It's time to bridge the gap and build leaders who think beyond tasks to drive vision, innovation, and growth." —
Jamie Anne Gustafson

It was 2009, Balad, Iraq, and I landed in this desert. I had experienced several difficult weeks, one that saw my then seven-year-old son drop me off at the airport where I boarded a plane with tears running down my face, sobbing next to a stranger, to processing and then moving on to my final destination, Balad, Iraq. I was among strangers and did not have anyone I knew. Looking for direction, I relied on my superiors. Yet when I reached out, I found a place characterized by gossip, false accusations, and a lack of concern. These leaders had many stripes yet failed to notice that I was in the wrong living arrangements and working in an area where I was struggling. I had arrived believing in the system, yet two things stood out to me at this moment—I was the only one I could rely on to ensure my needs were met, and two, I had been sold a false narrative about the values of the leadership and team.

I know this experience may have been unique to me. Yet when I left the military sector and continued my other career, I observed the same pattern. My leaders were not equipped to lead, and many lacked the desire to lead beyond a pay raise. This gap has continued to grow and has become evident during difficult times. A system crash highlighted this at the insurance company I worked for. The leaders shook their heads, failed to act, and felt they lacked the agency to address it, while those below them in the hierarchy took action to find a solution. The manager believed it was not his job. The overall value of the customers and team did not weigh heavily on him, and he had not been given the answers. So, customers became upset, and employees struggled.

It would not take you long to identify a leader you worked with who should not be in a position to guide or build. I do not fully blame the leader, as many don't feel they have a choice in the matter. The next step in most people's careers is management. This ladder is not designed to build and find the best person for the leadership position. Some of the greatest practitioners are not adept at taking the next rung on the ladder, nor do they really want to.

This concept hit home with me when I was deployed in a war zone. In the military, rank matters. During times of peace, it is easier to slip unnoticed and either fail to make decisions as a leader or neglect your people. However, during war or crisis, it is more than evident who caves under pressure, who leads with strength, and who values the team.

WHY THIS MATTERS

Leadership should be intentional, and grooming a leader should be built on the development of a strategic mindset. This matters because people matter—a salesman does not become a great leader simply because they are great at sales. We also have to highlight that we value expertise and do not punish our people by taking away something they are good at to focus on areas they may have no desire or aptitude for.

We have to reframe these concepts. Let practitioners build a pathway to success by improving their craft. Develop leaders based on aptitude, strategic thinking, and a desire to serve. Organizations, people, customers, and other stakeholders will emerge stronger on the other side by intentionally developing leadership. As an airman, I felt let down by the system, and, furthermore, I checked out as a team player and as a worker. I no longer trusted my mission, my team, or my personal trajectory.

CORE CONCEPT & FRAMEWORK

Imagine a world where we create space for true growth, where we allow for the setbacks that come with trying new things, and where stakeholders believe their growth can be connected to organizational success. It is no longer about blind faith but about creation. We all understand that any tech needs information to operate. No good customer management system can operate blindly. Yet we fail to view people the same way. A practice of work is different from the leadership of people and systems and requires different operating structures and information.

To lead themselves and others, people must understand what a strategic mindset is and how to cultivate it. If the failure of leadership is a failure of the process of leadership, then rebuilding it is the answer, and creating a whole new mindset. A strategic leader can see the full picture and understands that processing and enduring failure, frustration, and feedback are the only ways to drive forward movement for themselves and the organization.

THE ACCIDENTAL LEADER: WHEN TENURE TRUMPS TALENT

In my early career, I worked in an organization where leadership wasn't earned through vision, skill, or the ability to inspire others. Instead, it was distributed based on a single metric—time served. If you had been there long enough, you were promoted. It didn't matter if you had the aptitude to lead, the desire to develop others, or the ability to think strategically. Leadership was treated as a reward for tenure, not as a responsibility to guide, grow, and innovate.

At first, I didn't question it. I was new, eager to learn, and assumed that those in leadership roles had earned their positions through merit. I believed they were there to teach, to guide, and to help me grow. But it didn't take long for me to realize that wasn't the case.

My manager, let's call him Mark, had been with the organization for over a decade. He was promoted to a leadership role because, well, it was his turn. Mark wasn't a bad person. He was reliable, punctual, and knew the ins and outs of the job. But he wasn't a leader.

Mark's approach to leadership was purely transactional. He focused on tasks, deadlines, and metrics, but he didn't invest in his team. He didn't ask about our career goals, didn't provide feedback or mentorship, and didn't seem to care about anything beyond the immediate deliverables.

For someone like me, who was eager to learn and grow, this was devastating. I wanted to understand the "why" behind our work. I wanted to ask questions, share ideas, and contribute in meaningful ways. However, my questions went unanswered. My insights were ignored. My strengths were never acknowledged.

It became clear that my development stopped where I was. The only impact that mattered was the predefined metrics that affected Mark and his boss. My growth, my potential, my desire to contribute beyond the basics, none of it mattered.

One project in particular stands out in my memory. We were tasked with implementing a new process that would streamline operations and improve efficiency. It was a big undertaking, and I was excited to contribute. I had ideas, insights, and a genuine desire to make a difference.

Instead of engaging the team, Mark treated the project as a checklist. He assigned tasks without providing context, avoided team discussions, and dismissed any suggestions that didn't align with his narrow view of success.

I quickly realized that my role was not to think, innovate, or grow— it was to show up, do what was asked, and clock the hours. Anything beyond that was seen as unnecessary or even disruptive.

The breaking point for me came during a one-on-one meeting with Mark. I had prepared a list of questions and ideas, hoping to spark a conversation about my development and how I could contribute more effectively to the team.

As I started to share, Mark cut me off. "Just focus on what's in front of you," he said. "We don't need to overcomplicate things."

In that moment, I realized that my growth wasn't just being ignored; it was being actively stifled. Mark didn't see me as a future leader or even as someone with potential. To him, I was just another employee, there to fulfill a predefined role and nothing more.

I left that job not long after. I knew I couldn't thrive in an environment where my strengths weren't valued, my insights weren't heard, and my growth wasn't a priority.

Looking back, I wonder if Mark felt the same way. What if Mark didn't want to be a leader? What if he had been promoted not because he was ready or willing, but because the system demanded it? What if Mark's true potential wasn't in managing people, but in growing his craft?

The failure wasn't just in Mark's leadership—it was in the process that put him there. The system assumed that the next step for a high-performing employee was management, without considering whether that was the right path for them. It didn't offer alternative growth opportunities or recognize that leadership is a practice in itself, requiring its own set of skills, mindset, and intentional development.

What if, instead of promoting Mark to a leadership role, the organization had offered him a different growth opportunity? What if they had created a pathway for him to deepen his expertise, innovate in his field, and contribute at a higher level without managing people? What if leadership wasn't seen as the only way to advance, but as a distinct practice that required intentional preparation and a desire to serve others?

Imagine if Mark had been given the chance to grow in his craft. He could have become a subject matter expert, a mentor to others in his field, or an innovator driving new ideas and solutions. He could have thrived in a role that aligned with his strengths and passions, rather than struggling in one that didn't.

Imagine if leadership itself had been treated as a practice, a discipline that required training, mentorship, and ongoing development. What if the organization had identified individuals with the aptitude and desire to lead, and invested in their growth before promoting them? What if leadership formation were intentional, focused on building strategic thinkers who could guide, inspire, and innovate?

The accidental leader problem is not a failure of individuals; it's a failure of the process. When organizations treat leadership as the default next step, they create a cycle of unprepared leaders and disengaged teams. But when they offer alternative growth pathways and invest in intentional leadership formation, they create a culture where everyone can thrive.

Mark's story, and mine, are reminders of what happens when the process fails. They're also reminders of what's possible when the process succeeds. Leadership isn't about surviving the moment—it's about shaping the future. And that starts with rethinking how we define, develop, and value leadership.

DUAL WIFM LENSES (WHAT'S IN IT FOR ME?)

For leaders, this approach changes everything. Leadership is more than managing tasks; it is about building teams that are engaged, capable, and aligned with the bigger picture. Stronger teams lead to better results, and when people are placed in roles that match their strengths, they thrive. Offering growth opportunities outside of traditional leadership roles keeps top talent engaged, even if they do not want to manage others. Promotions based on skill and readiness, rather than time served, create better outcomes for everyone. Leaders who are prepared and strategic make smarter decisions, inspire their teams, and foster a culture where people want to stay and grow.

For employees, this approach creates new opportunities. When strengths are recognized and ideas are valued, it feels like you truly matter. Growth does not have to mean becoming a manager. It can mean becoming an expert, innovating in your field, or mentoring others. Leadership is not just about having a title; it is about taking ownership of your work, sharing ideas, and making an impact.

When given the tools to grow, whether through feedback, training, or new challenges, confidence and credibility naturally follow. For those who aspire to leadership, this approach ensures readiness when the time comes. Working in a place that values growth and contributions creates an environment where employees can truly thrive.

Making this happen does not require a complete overhaul, just a shift in how growth is approached. Leaders can start by rethinking the career ladder. Not every high performer needs to become a manager. Instead, create pathways for people to grow in ways that match their strengths, whether through deepening their expertise, innovating, or mentoring others. Investing in development through training, mentorship, and feedback ensures that when someone assumes a leadership role, they are prepared. Taking the time to listen to the team—understanding their goals, strengths, and what excites them—aligns individual growth with the organization's success.

When leadership development is intentional, everyone benefits. Leaders are better prepared to guide and inspire, employees feel valued and empowered, and organizations thrive with engaged, capable people driving success. This is not merely about fixing a broken system. It is about creating a culture in which growth, innovation, and collaboration are foundational. Leadership is not about just getting through the day; it is about shaping the future. When done right, everyone moves forward together.

From "Leadership Skills" to "Leadership Formation"

Shared accountability begins with small, intentional steps that create a ripple effect. Both leaders and employees have a role to play in building a culture of leadership formation, and it starts with clear actions and open dialogue.

Leader Action

Take time to identify one team member's unique strength or skill and find a way to highlight or leverage it in their current role.

Employee Action

Take an inward look and identify your strengths. Think about times when you felt you were firing on all cylinders and identify other areas that could leverage your uniqueness.

Conversation Prompt

"What is one way you could help change the system or your own growth to be deliberate in leadership formation?"

Small assessments like these create momentum and set the stage for a culture where ownership thrives. Leaders and employees working together in this way build trust, accountability, and shared success.

2

OWNERSHIP IS NOT A TITLE

"Ownership is not a title; it's the responsibility to shape outcomes and contribute to the bigger picture with long-term purpose in mind." —Jamie Anne Gustafson

I care about this outcome because I am connected to the systems and processes. I care about this outcome because I helped build it and want to be there to adjust.

Recently, I worked with a company preparing to sell (Company A), and the experience revealed a striking disconnect in the purchaser's (Company B) philosophy and approach to leadership. Succession planning is always a fascinating process to observe because it brings ownership to the forefront. It's a time when agendas surface, and the different drivers of each party come into play. In this case, Company B's leadership held a rigid belief system that clashed with Company A's very nature.

Company B believed outcomes could be achieved solely through rigid systems and automation, thereby eliminating the need for individual ownership or adaptability. To them, success was a matter of following processes rather than empowering people to take responsibility for results. While this approach might seem efficient on the surface, it revealed a critical flaw: without ownership of outcomes, the company lacked the agility and innovation needed to thrive in a fast-changing market.

Ownership isn't just about accountability. It's about creating a culture where individuals feel connected to the results of their work. It's about empowering people to think strategically, adapt to challenges, and take initiative when the unexpected arises. This company's reliance on rigid systems and rules stifled that sense of ownership, leaving its team ill-equipped to navigate the complexities of its industry.

At the heart of Company A's business was thought leadership, the crux of their assets. It wasn't the rigid systems or processes that would propel them forward, but the ability to innovate, adapt, and think critically about outcomes. Thought leadership requires more than execution—it demands ownership. It's the willingness to take responsibility for results, to adjust when things don't go as planned, and to continuously refine strategies to meet evolving needs.

This isn't just a lesson for one company or one industry; it's a universal truth. Ownership of outcomes is the engine of innovation and the key to long-term success. Systems and automation can enhance efficiency, but they cannot replace the human drive to take responsibility, solve problems, and push boundaries. Without ownership, companies risk stagnation, clinging to the belief that processes alone can deliver results.

Ultimately, Company B's failure to embrace ownership left it at a crossroads. They had the potential to thrive, but their unwillingness to empower their team to take responsibility for outcomes held them back. It was a powerful reminder that, in every industry, ownership isn't just about accountability but about creating space for people to innovate, adapt, and deliver results. Without it, even the most sophisticated systems fall short, and the opportunity for true progress is lost.

WHY THIS MATTERS

Ownership is at the heart of great leadership and healthy organizations. It is not just about being responsible for tasks but about feeling connected to the outcomes and having the freedom to shape them. When people take ownership, they start thinking strategically, acting with purpose, and contributing to something bigger than themselves. It is not about titles or authority; it is about behaviors that spark innovation, adaptability, and long-term success.

When organizations fail to encourage ownership, they often end up with a culture of compliance. People follow the rules, check the boxes, and do what they are told, but they are not invested in the results. This kind of environment stifles creativity, slows down progress, and, most importantly, fails to create leaders. Compliance-based cultures teach people to wait for instructions rather than take initiative. They discourage decision-making, problem-solving, and the kind of forward-thinking that leadership requires.

Without ownership, individuals never develop the confidence or skills to step into leadership roles. They become overly reliant on systems, processes, or top-down directives, leaving them unprepared to handle challenges or adapt to change. Instead of growing into leaders, they remain task-doers, unable to see the bigger picture or take responsibility for driving outcomes.

On the flip side, when people are encouraged to take ownership early through decision-making, confidence-building, and empowerment, they naturally become leaders, even before they hold formal titles. Ownership inspires people to step up, solve problems, and take action when needed. These behaviors drive innovation and help organizations thrive, especially in fast-changing industries.

Leadership is not something that comes with a title. It is built through actions and behaviors. Organizations that focus on fostering ownership create workplaces where people feel connected to their work, motivated to solve challenges, and ready to lead. Ownership gives people a sense of purpose and helps them see how their efforts contribute to the bigger picture.

This is important for the health of any organization. Companies that encourage ownership create a culture where people are not just doing their jobs—they are invested in the success of the whole team. This leads to better decisions, more creativity, and a workforce that can handle change and uncertainty. Ownership also makes organizations less dependent on rigid systems or top-down management, because the people within the organization are empowered to think and act independently.

Ownership is what drives progress. It is the bridge between having a vision and making it happen. Without it, even the best systems and processes will fall short. Without ownership, organizations fail to develop the next generation of leaders, leaving them vulnerable to stagnation and unprepared for the future. With it, organizations unlock the full potential of their people, creating a culture of leadership, innovation, and long-term success. This is why ownership matters—not just for individuals, but for the future of the entire organization.

CORE CONCEPT & FRAMEWORK

Ownership is often stifled when leaders are promoted based on tenure, technical skills, or time in a role, rather than on their ability to lead. While technical expertise and experience are undeniably valuable, they do not inherently translate into leadership qualities such as vision, adaptability, emotional intelligence, and the ability to inspire and empower others. Promotions based solely on these factors can create a leadership gap, where individuals in leadership roles lack the mindset and behaviors needed to foster ownership within their teams. This approach reinforces a culture of compliance, where people focus on fulfilling tasks and following instructions rather than taking initiative, thinking strategically, or driving meaningful outcomes. When leadership is treated as a reward for time served rather than as a responsibility to empower others and drive progress, ownership is stifled at every level of the organization. This not only limits individual growth but also hinders the organization's ability to innovate and adapt to change.

Participative ownership, on the other hand, thrives in organizations that encourage collaboration, shared responsibility, and decision-making, even among those without formal authority. It often appears informally in environments where people feel safe contributing and where their input is genuinely valued. For example, a team member might step up to solve a problem or take the lead on a project because they are passionate about the outcome, not because they were explicitly told to do so. Similarly, cross-functional teams might come together to address challenges or brainstorm solutions without waiting for directives from leadership. These informal displays of ownership are the seeds of leadership, and they flourish in cultures that prioritize empowerment, trust, and open communication over rigid hierarchies. When people feel their contributions matter and they have the freedom to act, they naturally take ownership of their work and the outcomes they influence.

Introducing the idea of ownership before authority is a transformative way to cultivate leadership behaviors early in an individual's career. Leadership is not about holding a title or formal power. It's about taking responsibility, driving outcomes, and inspiring others to do the same. Encouraging individuals to take ownership of their work and decisions helps them develop the confidence, skills, and mindset needed to lead, long before they step into formal leadership roles. This can be achieved by creating opportunities for team members to lead projects, make decisions, and solve problems within their areas of influence. For instance, a team member might be asked to present a solution to a challenge, lead a small initiative, or mentor a colleague. These experiences not only build critical skills like decision-making, problem-solving, and communication but also instill a sense of accountability and purpose. When individuals are given the chance to take ownership, they begin to see themselves as leaders, regardless of their formal position.

Introducing ownership before authority also shifts the focus from hierarchy to behavior. Leadership becomes something that people practice every day, rather than something they wait to be granted through a promotion. This approach creates a culture where everyone feels empowered to contribute to the organization's success, regardless of their role or title. It fosters a sense of shared responsibility, motivating people to take initiative and drive outcomes by connecting them to the bigger picture. For example, a junior employee who takes ownership of a project might inspire their peers to do the same, creating a ripple effect of proactive behavior and engagement. Over time, this culture of participative ownership strengthens the organization, ensuring that leadership is not confined to a select few but is distributed across the entire team. This not only enhances the organization's ability to innovate and adapt but also builds resilience by ensuring that leadership behaviors are embedded across all levels.

Organizations that prioritize ownership over authority break free from the limitations of traditional promotion models, which often reward tenure or technical skills over leadership potential. Instead, they create a leadership pipeline that is driven by behaviors—such as initiative, accountability, and strategic thinking—rather than by time served or technical expertise alone. This approach ensures that leaders at every level are equipped to inspire, empower, and drive progress. It also creates a more dynamic and engaged workforce, where individuals feel valued and motivated to contribute to the organization's success. When ownership is prioritized, people are not just doing their jobs. They are actively invested in the outcomes and the organization's future.

This intentional focus on ownership transforms the way organizations develop leaders. It ensures that leadership is not seen as a reward for past performance but as a responsibility to drive future progress. Leaders who have developed ownership behaviors before stepping into formal roles are better prepared to inspire their teams, navigate challenges, and adapt to change. They understand that leadership is about empowering others, not just about making decisions or giving orders. This creates a culture where leadership is distributed, innovation is encouraged, and the collective efforts of the entire organization drive progress.

When ownership precedes authority, it becomes the foundation for a thriving, resilient organization. Individuals at all levels feel empowered to take initiative, solve problems, and contribute to the bigger picture. This not only prepares them for future leadership roles but also ensures the organization continues to move forward, driven by a culture of shared responsibility and proactive engagement. Ownership becomes the engine of progress, transforming not just individuals but the entire organization into a dynamic, innovative, and future-ready entity.

LEADERSHIP STARTS LONG BEFORE AUTHORITY

When Alex joined their team, he was just another junior member in a group tasked with fixing a process that had been causing delays for months. No one expected Alex to take the lead. He didn't have a title, seniority, or formal authority. Something about the team's approach made Alex feel he could step up.

Instead of waiting for instructions, Alex dove in. He started by gathering data, talking to colleagues, and identifying bottlenecks that were slowing progress. Alex didn't wait for someone to assign him a task or tell him what to do. When the team met to discuss progress, Alex presented his findings and proposed a plan. It wasn't perfect, but it was thoughtful, and it got the ball rolling.

The team rallied around Alex's ideas, refining them together and ultimately implementing changes that saved time and reduced frustration for everyone involved. What's more, Alex's initiative inspired others on the team to step up as well. People began sharing their ideas, collaborating more openly, and taking ownership of their parts of the process. The team didn't just fix the problem. They became more engaged, more innovative, and more cohesive in the process.

What made Alex step up? It wasn't a directive from leadership or a formal promotion. It was the team's culture. The environment encouraged ownership. People were trusted to make decisions, take risks, and learn from the outcomes. Alex didn't need a title to lead. He just needed the space to act and present ideas.

This is what happens when ownership is cultivated early. Leadership behaviors like taking initiative, solving problems, and thinking strategically emerge naturally when people feel empowered to contribute. Alex's story isn't unique. It's a glimpse into what's possible when organizations prioritize ownership over compliance.

Now, imagine a different scenario. In some organizations, ownership is stifled. Promotions are often based on tenure or technical skills, and leadership is treated as a reward for time served rather than a responsibility to empower others. In these environments, people stick to their tasks, waiting for direction instead of stepping up. Compliance becomes the norm, and innovation stalls.

In these organizations, someone like Alex might have hesitated to act. He might have thought, "It's not my place," or "I'll wait for someone else to take the lead." Without a culture that encourages ownership, Alex's potential to lead would have gone untapped, and the team would have missed the improvements and energy his initiative would have brought.

The difference between these two scenarios comes down to how organizations design their cultures. In Alex's case, the team operated with trust and communication. Leaders set clear expectations but didn't micromanage. They celebrated not only successes but also the lessons learned from mistakes and/or understanding that failure is part of any process. This created an environment where people felt safe to take risks and make decisions.

Ownership doesn't just happen. It's built intentionally. It starts with giving people opportunities to lead before they have formal authority. For example, Alex's team didn't wait for a manager to assign leadership roles. Instead, they created space for anyone to step up, contribute ideas, and take responsibility for outcomes.

Organizations that prioritize ownership create environments where leadership behaviors thrive. This starts with designing systems that encourage decision-making at all levels. Leaders can set clear expectations, provide guidance without micromanaging, and celebrate success while still learning from every decision. Communication is key. Team members need to feel they can take risks, make mistakes, and, at times, fail without fear of harsh repercussions. Furthermore, failures are met with celebration of the pivot.

When ownership is encouraged, it transforms the way people approach their work. They stop seeing themselves as task-doers and start seeing themselves as contributors to the organization's success. This shift in mindset creates a ripple effect, inspiring individuals to take initiative, solve problems, and think strategically. Over time, this culture of participative ownership strengthens the organization, ensuring that leadership is not confined to a select few but is distributed across the entire team.

The key to avoiding a culture of compliance is to introduce leadership behaviors before leadership roles. Providing early-career professionals with opportunities to lead projects, solve problems, and collaborate builds confidence, decision-making skills, and a sense of accountability. These are the ingredients of great leadership.

Organizations that focus on building ownership unlock the full potential of their people. Teams become more engaged, creative, and adaptable. Leadership behaviors spread across the organization, creating a ripple effect that drives progress and innovation.

Alex's story shows what's possible when ownership is encouraged early. Leadership doesn't start with a title. It starts with a decision. When organizations create environments where people feel empowered to make those decisions, they build a culture of ownership that fuels long-term success.

Every decision someone makes today is a step toward becoming a leader. Organizations that embrace this approach create workplaces where leadership isn't just a title. It's a behavior that drives progress, inspires teams, and shapes the future.

Leadership begins long before authority, and it starts with creating environments where ownership is encouraged, supported, and celebrated. When organizations design for ownership, they don't just create better teams. They create better leaders, better outcomes, and a better future.

DUAL WIFM LENSES (WHAT'S IN IT FOR ME?)

Ownership is the foundation of both personal and organizational growth. For leaders, encouraging ownership early allows them to step back from micromanaging and focus on strategy, while empowering their teams to take initiative and solve problems independently. For employees, taking ownership builds confidence, credibility, and a sense of purpose, connecting their daily work to the bigger picture and unlocking opportunities for growth. Together, this creates a culture where leadership behaviors thrive at every level, driving innovation, engagement, and long-term success.

Leader Lens: Why This Matters Upstream

Encouraging ownership early transforms how leaders manage their teams. When employees take initiative and solve problems independently, leaders can step back from micromanaging and focus on strategy and long-term goals. This shift not only improves efficiency but also empowers teams to thrive.

Trusting employees to take ownership also boosts engagement and retention. When people feel valued and trusted, they are more likely to stay and contribute meaningfully. This creates a more cohesive and motivated team, reducing turnover and strengthening the organization.

Fostering ownership helps leaders identify and develop future leaders. When leaders encourage strategic behaviors before formal roles, managers can build a strong pipeline of high-potential employees who are ready to step into greater responsibilities.

Teams that embrace ownership also make better decisions. Proactive problem-solving and diverse perspectives lead to more innovative and effective outcomes that benefit the entire organization. Leaders who prioritize ownership create a culture of empowerment, trust, and long-term success.

Employee Lens: Why This Matters on the Ground

Taking ownership builds credibility and confidence. When employees make decisions and take responsibility for outcomes, they earn the trust of their peers and leaders. Each decision, whether successful or a learning experience, strengthens their influence and self-assurance.

Ownership allows employees to demonstrate leadership behaviors before they have a formal title. By stepping up, solving problems, and thinking strategically, they demonstrate readiness for greater responsibilities and future leadership roles.

Employees who take ownership unlock growth opportunities. Leaders are more likely to trust them with new challenges, giving them the chance to expand their skills, influence, and career potential.

Ownership also fosters a sense of purpose. Knowing their contributions matter connects employees to the bigger picture, motivating them to go above and beyond.

Practicing ownership prepares employees for leadership. Behaviors like accountability, adaptability, and decision-making are developed through action, equipping them with the skills needed to lead effectively in the future.

APPLICATION: TURNING INSIGHT INTO PRACTICE

Encouraging ownership early doesn't require massive overhauls or rigid systems. It calls for small, meaningful shifts in how people work together. It starts with everyday actions. Employees can ask themselves, "What can I do to move this forward?" instead of waiting for instructions or permission. This simple mindset shift has a profound impact, empowering individuals to take initiative and see themselves as contributors to the bigger picture. Leaders play a key role, stepping back and giving their teams the space to make decisions. Focusing on effort, learning, and progress rather than just outcomes reinforces the idea that taking action, even imperfect action, is valuable.

Decision-making begins to look different in a culture of ownership. Trusting people to make choices within clear boundaries encourages them to take initiative and experiment with new ideas. Leaders don't need to disappear or stop guiding their teams, but they can shift their focus to providing context, resources, and support. Sharing the "why" behind decisions and equipping teams with the tools they need creates an environment where employees feel confident solving problems and learning from the process. This approach not only builds decision-making skills but also fosters accountability and pride in the work.

Small shifts in behavior and decision-making ripple out across the organization, creating a culture where ownership thrives. People who feel safe taking risks and know they won't be punished for mistakes are more likely to innovate and demonstrate resilience. Teams become more engaged, proactive, and willing to tackle challenges head-on. Over time, this creates a steady pipeline of future leaders who are already practicing the skills they'll need in formal roles. Leadership becomes less about titles and more about behaviors, and the organization benefits from having leadership embedded at every level.

The beauty of this approach lies in its simplicity. Rigid rules or complicated systems aren't necessary. Trust, initiative, and learning become part of the culture, creating an environment where people feel empowered to act. Leaders don't need to have all the answers or control every decision. Instead, they can focus on empowering their teams, encouraging experimentation, and celebrating growth.

Organizations that embrace this mindset unlock the full potential of their people. Employees feel more connected to their work, more confident in their abilities, and more willing to step up when opportunities arise. Leaders, in turn, benefit from having teams that are engaged, innovative, and capable of driving progress. This creates a workplace where leadership starts long before anyone gets a title, and where everyone feels empowered to contribute to the organization's success.

PUTTING OWNERSHIP INTO PRACTICE

Encouraging ownership doesn't require a complete overhaul of systems or processes. It's about creating shared accountability and providing just enough structure to empower both leaders and employees to take meaningful action. Here's how to start putting ownership into practice right away:

Leader Action

Identify one area where your team can take more ownership and step back to let them lead. For example, assign a team member to lead a small project or decision, and provide them with the context and resources they need to succeed. Resist the urge to micromanage. Focus on supporting and guiding them instead.

Employee Action

Start practicing ownership by looking for opportunities to solve problems or take initiative, even in small ways. For instance, if you notice a process that could be improved, propose a solution or take the first step to address it. Show that you're invested in the outcome, not just the task.

Conversation Prompt

Leaders and employees can use this question to spark a dialogue about ownership:

"What's one area where you feel you could take more responsibility or make a bigger impact, and how can I support you in doing that?"

This approach reinforces buy-in on both sides. Leaders demonstrate trust and empower their teams, while employees build confidence and develop leadership behaviors. Over time, these small actions create a culture where ownership is not just encouraged but expected, driving innovation, engagement, and long-term success.

Ownership lays the groundwork for leadership, but the journey doesn't stop there. True growth often emerges from navigating the challenges that ownership brings—frustration, failure, and feedback. These forces, while uncomfortable, are some of the most powerful developmental tools available.

Taking ownership inevitably leads to obstacles. Frustration surfaces when plans don't unfold as expected, failure occurs when risks fall short, and feedback pushes individuals to confront assumptions and strive for improvement. These moments are not setbacks—they are opportunities to build resilience, adaptability, and the ability to learn from experience. These qualities are at the heart of great leadership.

The next chapter explores how frustration, failure, and feedback shape individuals and teams. These forces are part of the process, not something to avoid. Environments that encourage people to fail safely, reflect openly, and grow intentionally unlock the full potential of their teams. Let's explore how these developmental forces transform ownership into leadership.

PART TWO
THE CONDITIONS THAT CREATE OWNERSHIP

3
THE THREE F'S: HOW PEOPLE ACTUALLY GROW

"True leadership isn't about fixing or rescuing. It's about calibrating growth, creating space for others to struggle, learn, and thrive." —Jamie Anne Gustafson

I had spent years in my business classes learning about this company and dreaming of one day working there. So, when a sales position opened, I jumped at the chance. The onboarding was impressive—thoughtful training, a warm welcome, and lessons on caring for customers and understanding the market. I felt like I was exactly where I belonged, and the first few months flew by. My managers celebrated my work, I received glowing reviews, and every day I felt a surge of excitement when I logged in.

Slowly, I started to notice cracks. There were strict ideas about what success looked like, and most of them had more to do with dashboard metrics than with actually helping customers. The space to be creative and to solve real problems for people felt smaller than I expected. If a customer had a tricky issue, I quickly realized how hard it was to get it fixed. Processes were broken, and going beyond your direct responsibility was discouraged. At first, I brushed it off. After a while, my enthusiasm started to wane. There was no room for failure or frustration, and there was little feedback to support my growth or benefit the customer. I wanted to guide customers to the right solution to make their lives better, but I found myself constrained by a checklist of metrics that made little difference to them.

Instead of feeling empowered, I was acting in a kind of theater, ticking off tasks, meeting quotas, but not truly making a difference. It was disappointing, and some days it was even discouraging. I was not allowed to use all the tools I'd been trained on or bring in fresh ideas because following the process mattered more than finding a real solution. That is when I realized—no matter the talent or training, without room to think and act, people can't truly grow. It is the heart of what this chapter explores—what happens when good intentions get boxed in, and what it really takes to create the conditions for ownership and meaningful growth.

WHY THIS MATTERS

Fostering organizational and personal agency is essential for building resilient, innovative teams and confident, self-directed leaders. At its core, agency is about empowering individuals to take ownership of their actions, decisions, and outcomes, while creating an environment where teams feel trusted to act, experiment, and grow. Frustration, failure, and feedback—the three "F words" —are not obstacles to avoid but the catalysts that make agency possible. Together, they form a powerful cycle of growth that transforms challenges into opportunities.

Frustration is often the first signal that growth is on the horizon. It arises when there's a gap between where someone is and where they want to be, pushing individuals to think critically, solve problems, and take initiative. For individuals, frustration builds resilience and confidence, encouraging them to take ownership of challenges rather than waiting for direction. For organizations, frustration highlights inefficiencies or unmet needs, sparking innovation and driving teams to find better solutions. When reframed as a natural part of progress, frustration becomes a gateway to growth.

Failure is also an inevitable part of any new or changing process. It's not just a possibility; it's a necessary step in the journey of growth and innovation. Failure teaches individuals to navigate uncertainty, adapt to unexpected outcomes, and refine their approaches. It builds resilience by showing that setbacks are not the end of the road but opportunities to learn and improve. For organizations, failure provides valuable insights into what works and what doesn't, helping teams iterate and innovate. Leaders who normalize failure create environments where people feel safe to take risks, experiment, and grow. When failure is embraced as part of the process, it reduces fear, increases engagement, and empowers individuals to act boldly.

Feedback is the bridge that connects frustration and failure to meaningful growth. It provides the clarity and actionable insights needed to refine approaches, improve performance, and build confidence. For individuals, feedback fosters self-awareness and highlights areas for growth, reinforcing their sense of agency. For organizations, feedback creates a culture of continuous improvement, where open communication and collaboration drive progress. When feedback is seen as a tool for learning rather than criticism, it strengthens both personal and organizational agency.

The interplay of frustration, failure, and feedback creates a powerful cycle of growth. Frustration pushes individuals to act, failure provides lessons to refine their approach, and feedback offers the insights needed to improve and iterate. Together, these forces build resilience, adaptability, and strategic thinking, key traits of both personal and organizational agency.

Leaders play a pivotal role in fostering agency through these forces. Calibrating frustration ensures it challenges individuals without overwhelming them. Normalizing failure encourages risk-taking and innovation. Encouraging feedback as a tool for growth creates an environment where people feel supported and empowered. Leaders who model these behaviors demonstrate that agency is not about perfection but about learning, adapting, and growing.

When frustration, failure, and feedback are embraced as part of the culture, individuals feel empowered to take ownership of their work and contribute meaningfully to the organization. Teams become more engaged, innovative, and resilient, driving the organization forward even amid uncertainty. Failure, frustration, and feedback are not roadblocks—they are stepping stones to success. Together, they create a culture where ownership, leadership, and growth thrive, ensuring that both individuals and organizations are prepared to navigate change and achieve lasting success.

CORE CONCEPT & FRAMEWORK

The core idea of this chapter is that **frustration, failure, and feedback**—the Three F's—are not obstacles but essential forces for growth, resilience, and innovation. When embraced and managed effectively, these forces empower individuals to take ownership, develop leadership skills, and foster a culture of continuous improvement within organizations. Frustration signals the edge of growth, pushing individuals and teams to problem-solve, adapt, and innovate. Failure is a natural part of any new or changing process, providing valuable lessons and opportunities to refine and improve. Feedback bridges frustration and failure, offering the clarity and insights needed to iterate, grow, and succeed. Together, the Three

F's create a powerful framework for building personal and organizational agency, turning challenges into stepping stones for success. This chapter explores how these forces manifest, their impact, and how to harness them for meaningful growth.

FORGED IN FRUSTRATION: HOW FAILURE AND FEEDBACK FUEL GROWTH

If I had to pinpoint the moments that shaped me the most, they wouldn't be the ones where everything went smoothly. Growth didn't happen when I had all the answers or when the path was clear. It happened in the messy, uncomfortable spaces where frustration, failure, and feedback collided. Those moments were neither glamorous nor easy, but they were transformative. Let me take you back to one of those times, a moment when I was thrown into the deep end and had to learn how to swim, even when I felt like I was drowning.

More than a decade ago, I started a new job with high hopes and clear expectations. I had a job description, a list of goals, and what I thought was a roadmap to success. I was ready to prove myself, to show that I could deliver results and make an impact. Within weeks, those expectations unraveled. My supervisor handed me what felt like a "long leash" and said, "Figure it out." That was it. No detailed instructions, no clear direction, no safety net. Just those three words. At first, I thought this freedom was empowering. I told myself, *This is my chance to shine. I'll figure it out, no problem.* As the days stretched on, that freedom started to feel more like abandonment. I had no clear direction, no structure, and no idea what success was supposed to look like. I felt like I was wandering in the dark, unsure of where I was going or how to get there.

Frustration set in—deep, gnawing frustration. I felt like I was failing every day, and I didn't even know what I was failing at. I wanted someone to step in, to give me the answers, to tell me what to do. No one did. I was on my own. I stumbled forward. I made mistakes, big ones. I tried things that didn't work. I built systems that fell apart. Every time I failed, I had to pick myself up and try again. It was exhausting. There were days when I questioned whether I was even cut out for the job. I wondered if I was in over my head, if I was destined to fail. Frustration, as it turns out, is a powerful teacher. It forces you to confront your own limitations, to dig deeper, to think harder. It pushes you to find solutions, even when you feel like giving up.

Failure is humbling. It strips away your ego and forces you to face the reality of what isn't working. It's also a powerful teacher. Every failure gave me data. Every misstep showed me what didn't work and nudged me closer to what might. Slowly, I started to see patterns. I began to understand the problems I was trying to solve. I learned to adapt, to iterate, to build something better with each attempt. Failure alone was not enough. What really pushed me forward was feedback.

Feedback came in many forms. Sometimes it was direct, an honest conversation with my supervisor or a colleague, pointing out where I'd gone wrong. Other times, it was indirect, the results of a project that didn't land the way I'd hoped or the silence that followed an idea that didn't resonate. At first, feedback stung. It felt like confirmation of my inadequacy, like a spotlight shining on all the ways I was not measuring up. Over time, I started to see it differently. Feedback was not a judgment. It was a tool. It was a mirror, showing me where I needed to grow. I learned to seek it out, to ask questions, to listen without defensiveness. Something remarkable happened. The frustration that had once felt paralyzing became a motivator. Failure became a stepping stone. Feedback became a guide. Together, they created a powerful cycle of growth.

Years later, when I became a leader, I thought I could spare my team the frustration I had endured. I built systems, created processes, and tried to eliminate ambiguity. I wanted to give them the clarity I had craved. I thought I was doing them a favor, giving them the tools I had wished for. I quickly realized that in my effort to protect them, I was holding them back. Without frustration, there was no urgency to solve problems. Without failure, there was no opportunity to learn. Without feedback, there was no growth. My team followed the systems I had created, but they didn't take initiative. They waited for direction instead of finding their own solutions. They relied on me for answers instead of developing the confidence to figure things out themselves. I had removed the very challenges that had shaped me, and in doing so, I had denied them the opportunity to grow.

That's when I realized my job wasn't to eliminate frustration, it was to calibrate it. True growth happens in the sweet spot between clarity and chaos. It's built when people have enough information to start, but not enough to finish without learning, adapting, and growing along the way. Frustration pushes us to dig deeper. Failure teaches us what doesn't work. Feedback indicates how to improve. Together, they create a powerful cycle of growth. As a leader, my role wasn't to provide all the answers. It was intended to create an environment in which frustration, failure, and feedback could do their work.

One of the ways I've embraced this philosophy is through something my team calls the "Celebration of the Pivot." In these meetings, we don't just celebrate successes; we celebrate the moments when things went wrong. We discuss what failed, why it failed, and how we adapted. We highlight the lessons learned and the solutions we created. These conversations have become a cornerstone of our culture. They remind us that failure isn't something to fear but something to learn from. They've taught us that the moments when things fall apart are often the moments when we grow the most.

Looking back, I'm grateful for every moment of frustration, every failure, and every piece of feedback I received. Those experiences didn't merely shape my career—they shaped me. They taught me resilience. They taught me to create clarity where none existed. They taught me that growth isn't linear, it's messy, uncomfortable, and often frustrating. Now, as a leader, I strive to offer that same gift to others. I guide them through frustration, helping them see that failure isn't the end, it's the beginning of something better. Frustration, failure, and feedback aren't obstacles to avoid. They're the foundation of growth. When we embrace them, we discover just how much we're capable of.

DUAL WIFM LENSES (WHAT'S IN IT FOR ME?)

Understanding the dynamics of growth, frustration, and failure isn't just a philosophical exercise. It has tangible implications for how we work and lead. To truly integrate these concepts, we need to examine them through two distinct lenses: the leader's upstream view and the employees' ground-level view. Here is how this shift translates into value for you.

Leader Lens: Why This Matters Upstream

For leaders, adopting this mindset requires a fundamental shift from being a "fixer" to becoming a "calibrator." Your value isn't defined by how many problems you solve for your team, but by how many problems you empower them to solve themselves. When you stop rescuing, you stop being the bottleneck for decision-making. You allow your team to build the muscle memory required to handle complex challenges without your constant intervention.

Top performers naturally crave autonomy. When you allow space for frustration and ownership, you create an environment where high-potential employees feel challenged and trusted. This deepens engagement and retention because your team knows they are developing real skills, not just following a manual. They stay because they are growing, not because the job is easy.

Finally, when you encourage your team to navigate failure and feedback, you get better data. You move away from theoretical planning and into practical iteration. Leaders who embrace this model foster teams that are agile, resilient, and capable of making sound decisions without constant oversight. You will notice a shift from employees asking, "What should I do?" to "Here is the underlying issue I see, or here is my proposed solution," signaling a maturing, high-performing culture.

Employee Lens: Why This Matters on the Ground

For employees, embracing the "long leash" is the fastest way to build credibility. When you stop waiting for instructions and start taking ownership of the gray areas, you demonstrate leadership potential before you even have the title. You demonstrate to your organization and yourself that you can handle ambiguity, a rare and valuable skill in any industry.

True confidence comes from surviving failure and solving hard problems, not from always getting it right the first time. When you navigate frustration and emerge with a solution, you build a reserve of self-trust. You know that no matter what challenge arises, you have the agency to figure it out. This shift in mindset transforms you from a passive participant to an active driver of your own career.

Leadership isn't a title—it's a behavior. When you are actively seeking feedback and treating frustration as a puzzle to be solved rather than a roadblock, you are practicing the exact skills you will need as a future leader. You are learning to calibrate your own growth, which is the first step toward eventually calibrating the growth of others. Ownership shows up before authority, and those who seize it are the ones who rise.

APPLICATION: TURNING INSIGHT INTO PRACTICE

We often talk about growth, resilience, and agency in abstract terms. While it's easy to agree that frustration signals opportunity, failure offers data, and feedback provides calibration, these ideas only become truly meaningful when we see how they play out in the everyday chaos of work, like a Tuesday morning when a project is off the rails and deadlines are looming.

Turning these insights into practice isn't about memorizing a new framework. It's about how we respond to the daily friction we encounter. Rather than defaulting to "fixing," the invitation is to shift into a mindset of "calibrating." For instance, the most significant behavioral shift comes when we stop trying to rescue others from struggle and instead act as a resource for their growth. This shift applies whether we lead a team or navigate our own career. When a problem arises and tension mounts, our instinct is often to jump in with solutions to reduce anxiety. However, inserting a "strategic pause" changes the dynamic—instead of immediately prescribing a fix, we ask, "What have you tried so far, and what is your next best guess?" This simple question compels others to use their own problem-solving muscles and signals trust in their ability to figure things out, even if they're still stuck.

Frustration, too, often triggers a defensive response, but practicing agency means vocalizing frustration as a neutral signal, not a negative emotion. Rather than falling into blame, "This is a mess— why can't we get this right?", it's more effective to name the gap: "I'm frustrated because there's a distance between our current output and the standard we need. Let's look at what's causing that gap." Naming the real issue moves the team from blame to diagnostics.

Embracing failure as usable data also shifts how decisions get made. The goal shifts from finding the "perfect" choice to finding the choice that will drive the fastest learning loop. Traditional decision-making encourages endless analysis to avoid mistakes, but a more useful question is, "Is this experiment safe to fail?" When a decision is reversible and failure's cost is manageable, taking action is usually worth it. If faced with two courses of action, choosing the one that'll yield concrete feedback sooner allows us to learn faster —the speed of learning outweighs the illusion of certainty.

Feedback should serve as a constant navigation tool, rather than a mechanism for annual or quarterly correction. Instead of reviewing progress only at preset intervals, it's helpful to adopt frequent "calibration checks." Asking, "What did we learn this week that challenges our assumptions?" creates space for course correction and prevents the sunk-cost fallacy of rigidly adhering to failing plans.

When these shifts in behavior and decision-making take hold, their effects ripple through the organization. The culture that emerges is less about compliance and more about agency—fewer people waiting for orders, and more people taking ownership. Problems get solved closer to the work, rather than always escalating to leadership. For this distributed problem-solving to work, leaders must become comfortable relinquishing the need to see and control every detail, trading some visibility for greater speed and agility across the team.

How an organization handles failure is another marker of its growth mindset. Hosting "blameless post-mortems" when projects go wrong keeps the focus on processes and systems, not individuals. Instead of asking who failed, we examine what failed in the approach—did we miss a signal or lack needed resources? This process builds psychological safety, encouraging people to take risks and innovate, knowing that honest mistakes won't bring punishment.

Applying these ideas in practice is never tidy. The balance of support and challenge won't be perfect every time. Over-calibration might leave someone floundering, while under-calibration can result in micromanagement. This is just part of the process of growth. The goal isn't instant perfection as a leader or employee, but to use each daily challenge as an experiment. Let frustration prompt mindful pauses, see failure as a source of new information, and treat feedback like a map for ongoing progress. Through these everyday shifts, abstract concepts of growth become tangible and enduring.

PUTTING OWNERSHIP INTO PRACTICE

Ownership thrives in environments where the Three F's—failure, frustration, and feedback—are embraced as opportunities for growth. Framing assignments around problems and outcomes rather than instructions allows employees to navigate challenges, learn from setbacks, and refine their approach. This approach builds trust and accountability while fostering the resilience and adaptability needed for long-term success.

Leader Action

Identify one upcoming project or assignment. Instead of explaining *how* to do it, frame the assignment by defining the *problem* and the desired *outcome*.

- **The Old Way:** "I need you to run a report on Q3 sales, put it in a slide deck, and email it to the team by Friday."
- **The Ownership Way:** "We need to understand why Q3 sales dipped in the Northeast region so we can adjust our Q4 strategy. Diagnose the issue and present your findings to the team by Friday. How you get there is up to you."

This approach transfers the cognitive load to the employee. It signals trust in their judgment and allows them to design the solution, thereby increasing their commitment to the outcome and opening the space for growth through the Three F's.

Employee Action

The next time you feel frustrated or sense that failure is near, pause and ask yourself—what feedback is this situation generating for me or others? How can I get ahead of it? Consider what your manager, your team, or even you might need in order to move forward constructively. This could mean initiating an honest conversation, sharing lessons learned, or seeking guidance before problems escalate.

Conversation Prompt

During your next one-on-one meeting, use this specific question to calibrate your working relationship:

"In what areas of your work do you feel you need more guidance from me, and in what specific areas are you ready to run entirely on your own?"

Failure, frustration, and meaningful feedback can only arise in environments where trust exists. The best way to build foundational trust is steadily through consistent actions during calm periods. This foundation is built on strategy, synergy, and systems, providing the framework for lasting growth and accountability.

4

THE FOUR S'S: HOW ORGANIZATIONS ENABLE OR KILL OWNERSHIP

"Strategy charts the course, Synergy unites the team, Systems ensure efficiency, and Stories inspire connection—together, these Four S's are the backbone of every thriving company." —Jamie Anne Gustafson

The CEO stepped to the front of the room, gripping the podium as he scanned the faces of his team. Months of work had gone into the slideshow behind him—charts, projections, and plans meticulously crafted to address the business's challenges. Sales were down, and everyone in the room understood the toll COVID had taken on their industry. Despite the setbacks, the business continued to move forward, inch by inch.

What no one in the room knew was that he had been preparing to step away. The thought had lingered in his mind for months. The business he had poured his heart into had changed and so had he. Years of putting out fires, chasing problems, and keeping the wheels turning had left him disconnected from the work he once loved. Somewhere along the way, the business had started running him— he was no longer running the business. He had been so consumed with managing day-to-day chaos that he failed to cultivate the next generation of leaders who could drive the company forward. Exhaustion had replaced passion, and he had convinced himself it was time to move on, to hand over the reins and walk away.

As he looked out at the room, something shifted. The faces staring back at him weren't just employees but people who had built this company alongside him. Families whose children he had watched grow up, colleagues who had weathered every storm with him, and a team that had become a second family. In that moment, he realized the driving motivation that had once fueled him hadn't disappeared. It was still there, buried beneath the cracks that had formed in the foundation of the business.

The problem wasn't the people, the market, or even the pandemic. The systems that had once propelled the company forward were no longer enough to sustain it. He had been so focused on keeping the business afloat that he had failed to adapt, to remodel the very framework that had brought them to this point. The cracks weren't a sign to abandon ship; they were a call to rebuild.

A choice was made in that room. Walking away wasn't the answer. Instead, he would lean in and rebuild the foundation with intention. Strategy would chart the course, synergy would unite the team, systems would ensure efficiency, and stories would inspire and connect. These weren't just abstract ideas—they were the pillars that had built the business and the people who made it thrive. He also knew that rebuilding meant empowering others, fostering a culture of shared leadership, and ensuring the business could continue to thrive without him at the helm.

This book is about people and leadership. It's about the hard truths and moments of clarity that define what it means to lead. A leader running in circles without a solid foundation, without strategy, systems, synergy, and stories, will burn out long before reaching the finish line. Leadership isn't about doing it all—it's about building something that lasts. The Four S's are the key to making that happen.

WHY THIS MATTERS

When a leader becomes consumed by the business instead of leading it, the cracks that form don't only impact the leader. They ripple through the entire organization. Strategy becomes reactive instead of proactive, systems break down under the weight of inefficiency, and the development of future leaders is neglected. This creates a dangerous cycle in which the business becomes overly dependent on a single person, leaving it vulnerable to stagnation or collapse when that leader inevitably burns out.

Ownership isn't just about keeping the lights on or putting out fires but building a sustainable foundation that allows the business to thrive beyond any one individual. Leadership development is critical to this process. Without cultivating the next generation of leaders, the organization lacks the visionaries and problem-solvers needed to adapt, grow, and innovate. A healthy organization is one where leadership is shared, systems are resilient, and the team is aligned around a clear purpose.

This matters because businesses that fail to prioritize strategy, systems, synergy, and storytelling often find themselves stuck in survival mode, unable to move forward. Thriving companies require leaders who don't just react to problems but create a vision for the future, align their teams around that vision, and build systems that ensure long-term success. Leadership isn't about doing it all; it's about empowering others, fostering collaboration, and creating a culture where the business can grow and evolve, no matter who is at the helm. Without this foundation, even the most passionate leader will tire, and the organization will falter.

CORE CONCEPT & FRAMEWORK

The foundation of every thriving company lies in the Four S's: **Strategy, Synergy, Systems, and Stories**. These interconnected drivers are essential for guiding growth, aligning teams, and creating lasting impact. Without them, leadership cannot truly form, no matter how motivated or passionate the individual. Structure enables ownership. Without a solid framework, even the most driven leaders will struggle to succeed.

Strategy provides the roadmap for success. It defines where the organization is now, where it wants to go, and how to get there. Without a strategy, efforts become scattered, and leaders are left reacting to problems instead of proactively driving the business forward. A clear strategy ensures every decision and action is aligned with a shared vision, giving leaders the clarity they need to lead effectively.

Synergy is the power of collaboration. It breaks down silos, fosters teamwork, and creates a culture where the whole is greater than the sum of its parts. Without synergy, teams become fragmented, and leaders are forced to shoulder the burden alone. True ownership thrives when collaboration is prioritized, allowing leaders to align their teams and harness collective strengths.

Systems are the backbone of efficiency and scalability. They provide the structure and processes that keep the business running smoothly, ensuring consistency and adaptability. But systems do more than maintain operations. They are also critical to developing strategic leaders. Strong systems create opportunities for leadership development by delegating responsibility, fostering decision-making, and providing clear frameworks for growth. Without these systems, leaders are left micromanaging or firefighting, unable to focus on the bigger picture. Systems that empower others to lead strategically ensure the organization is not dependent on a single individual but instead thrives through shared leadership and accountability.

Stories are the heart of connection. They humanize the brand, inspire employees, and build trust with customers. Without stories, leaders struggle to connect with their teams and customers on an emotional level, leaving the organization without a sense of purpose or identity. Stories bring the company's mission and values to life, creating the emotional resonance that drives engagement and loyalty.

Structure is the foundation of ownership. Without the Four S's—Strategy, Synergy, Systems, and Stories—leaders are left without the tools they need to succeed. Motivation alone cannot overcome a lack of structure, and without it, leadership falters, teams become disjointed, and the organization stagnates. When these Four S's are intentionally cultivated, they create a resilient, innovative, and purpose-driven organization where leadership thrives, and ownership flourishes.

BUILDING A FOUNDATION: HOW WILLOW FURNITURE TRANSFORMED THROUGH STRATEGY, SYNERGY, SYSTEMS, AND STORIES

When Willow Furniture first began, it was a small, family-run business with a simple mission: to create beautiful, high-quality furniture that made houses feel like homes. Cara and Sam, the founders, poured their hearts into every piece, crafting furniture that resonated with their local community. Word of their craftsmanship spread, and before long, the business grew. They expanded to online sales, opened a second showroom, and found themselves shipping their pieces across the country.

As the company grew, so did the challenges. Orders were delayed, communication between teams broke down, and customers began to feel like simply another transaction. Cara and Sam were overwhelmed. The business was running them—they weren't running the business. They were so focused on keeping up with demand that they had lost sight of their vision.

One evening, after yet another long day of putting out fires, Cara and Sam sat down at their kitchen table and made a decision. They would rebuild Willow Furniture from the ground up. They would focus on creating a strong foundation for the business, one that could sustain their growth and bring their original vision back to life. They didn't know it at the time, but this decision would lead them to what they would later call the Four S's: Strategy, Synergy, Systems, and Stories.

The first step was to create a clear strategy. Cara and Sam gathered their leadership team and asked three critical questions: Where are we now? Where do we want to go? How do we get there? They took an honest look at their strengths, such as their reputation for craftsmanship and loyal customer base, and their weaknesses, including inconsistent delivery times and a lack of leadership development. They set a bold but clear goal: to become the most trusted name in home furniture for families who value quality and sustainability.

To achieve this, they broke their vision into actionable steps. They would expand their product line to include customizable options, invest in sustainable materials, and improve their delivery process. One of the most critical parts of their strategy was building other leaders within the company. Cara and Sam realized that for Willow Furniture to thrive, they couldn't do it all themselves. They needed to create a culture in which leadership wasn't concentrated at the top but distributed throughout the organization.

They focused on leader formation by providing their team with three key elements: **information, space, and desire**. First, they ensured their employees had access to the necessary information to make decisions. This meant being transparent about the company's goals, sharing data openly, and providing training on everything from customer insights to financial literacy.

Next, they created space for employees to step into leadership roles. Cara and Sam encouraged their team to take ownership of projects, make decisions, and experiment with new ideas. They launched a mentorship program where experienced employees could guide newer team members, and they made it clear that mistakes were opportunities to learn, not reasons for punishment.

Finally, they focused on cultivating desire. Cara and Sam knew that leadership couldn't be forced—it had to come from within. They worked to inspire their team by connecting their daily work to the company's larger mission. They shared stories of how their furniture was transforming customers' homes and lives, and they celebrated the contributions of every employee, from the craftsman in the workshop to the delivery driver on the road.

One of the first employees to rise through this new approach was Elena, a customer service representative who had always gone above and beyond for clients. With the right information, the space to take on more responsibility, and the encouragement to lead, Elena quickly became a standout leader. She spearheaded a project to streamline customer communication, reducing response times and improving satisfaction. Within a year, she was promoted to head of client experience, where she mentored her own team and helped shape the company's future.

As they worked on their strategy, Cara and Sam realized that one of their biggest challenges was a lack of synergy. Departments operated in silos, and communication was often strained. The design team didn't understand the production team's challenges, and customer service felt disconnected from the rest of the company.

To address this, they started breaking down silos. Cross-departmental meetings became regular, and teams were encouraged to share their challenges and successes. They also launched the "Home Harmony Initiative," which paired employees from different departments to work on special projects together. One of the most impactful projects involved a designer who teamed up with a delivery driver to create a new packaging system that reduced transit damage. The program not only improved communication but also sparked innovation and strengthened relationships across the company.

As synergy grew, so did morale. Employees began to see themselves as part of a larger mission, and the company's culture shifted from fragmented to united.

While the team was coming together, Cara and Sam knew they still needed to address the lack of systems that were holding the business back. Processes were inconsistent, and too much institutional knowledge was locked in the heads of a few key employees. When their operations manager left unexpectedly, it caused chaos.

Sam took the lead on building systems that would bring clarity and efficiency to the business. They started by documenting every major process, from furniture production to customer service. They invested in a project management platform that allowed teams to track progress, share updates, and collaborate in real time.

The systems didn't just make the company more efficient—they created opportunities for growth and leadership at every level. Employees like Elena, who had stepped into leadership roles, now had the tools and support they needed to succeed.

As the business stabilized, Cara and Sam turned their attention to something they had neglected for far too long: their story. When they first started Willow Furniture, their passion for creating homes filled with warmth and comfort was at the heart of everything they did. As the company grew, that story had gotten lost. Customers loved their products, but they didn't always understand the "why" behind the brand.

To reconnect with their audience, they launched a storytelling campaign called "Homes We Build." The campaign featured real stories from customers, employees, and even the founders themselves. One video showed a young couple furnishing their first home with Willow Furniture pieces, sharing how the furniture made their space feel like their own. Another story highlighted a craftsman in the workshop who explained how he poured his heart into every piece he built.

Internally, stories became a way to inspire and align the team. At every company meeting, employees were invited to share "Willow Moments," examples of how their work had made a difference. These stories reminded everyone why they were there and reinforced the company's mission.

The storytelling campaign didn't just resonate with customers—it reignited the company's passion. Willow Furniture wasn't just selling furniture—it was helping people create homes filled with love and memories.

By focusing on the Four S's—Strategy, Synergy, Systems, and Stories—Willow Furniture transformed from a company struggling to keep up with its growth into a thriving, purpose-driven organization. Strategy gave them a clear roadmap and aligned their efforts toward a shared vision. Synergy fostered collaboration and innovation, breaking down silos and uniting the team. Systems created clarity, efficiency, and opportunities for leadership development. Stories connected them with their customers and reminded their team of their purpose.

Today, Willow Furniture is not just a furniture business—it is a company that inspires loyalty, innovation, and trust. The Four S's didn't just save the business—they became the foundation for its success. Cara and Sam's journey is a testament to the power of intentional leadership and the impact of building a strong foundation. When companies focus on the Four S's, they don't just survive, they thrive.

DUAL WIFM LENSES (WHAT'S IN IT FOR ME?)

The Four S's—Strategy, Synergy, Systems, and Stories—offer leaders a powerful framework to create clarity, alignment, and sustainable growth. This framework not only empowers teams to thrive but also builds a culture of collaboration, accountability, and purpose, ensuring the organization's success at every level.

Leader Lens: Why This Matters Upstream

The Four S's—Strategy, Synergy, Systems, and Stories—equips leaders and managers with a framework to create clarity, alignment, and sustainable growth. Leaders gain the ability to shift from reactive problem-solving to proactive leadership. A clear strategy ensures that teams are aligned around a shared vision, reducing wasted effort and enabling leaders to focus on innovation and long-term success rather than constant firefighting.

Fostering synergy transforms team dynamics and enhances decision-making by encouraging collaboration and breaking down silos. Teams that work together effectively generate better solutions and stronger results, reducing the pressure on individual leaders to shoulder the entire burden. Leaders who prioritize collaboration create an environment where collective strength drives success.

Strong systems provide the structure needed to delegate responsibility and identify emerging talent. These systems create opportunities for leadership development, ensuring that the organization is not overly reliant on a single individual. Leaders should pay attention to team members who take initiative, solve problems, and demonstrate ownership, as these individuals are often ready to grow into larger roles.

Stories offer leaders a way to inspire and connect with their teams on a deeper level. Sharing the company's mission, values, and successes creates a sense of purpose that motivates employees and builds trust. Leaders who tell authentic, emotionally resonant stories can unite their teams and foster engagement, making the organization stronger and more cohesive.

Employee Lens: Why This Matters on the Ground

The Four S's unlock opportunities for employees to grow their credibility, confidence, and influence. A clear strategy helps employees understand how their work contributes to the company's larger goals, providing a sense of direction and purpose. Seeing the direct impact of their efforts builds confidence and strengthens their connection to the organization's success.

Synergy creates an environment where employees can collaborate across teams, share ideas, and learn from one another. This fosters a sense of belonging and allows employees to build relationships that enhance their visibility and credibility. Contributions are recognized and valued, which helps employees feel more engaged and appreciated.

Ownership becomes possible when systems provide the tools and structure needed to take responsibility for work. Employees who step up to solve problems, improve processes, or mentor colleagues demonstrate leadership qualities that set them apart. These actions prepare employees for future leadership roles and create opportunities for recognition and advancement.

Stories inspire employees by connecting their daily work to the company's mission and values. Hearing how their efforts have made a difference—whether through a customer's success or a team's innovative solution—reinforces a sense of purpose. Sharing personal stories, such as leading a project or overcoming a challenge, builds confidence and influence within the organization.

Aspiring leaders can focus on behaviors like taking initiative, being accountable, and collaborating effectively. Leadership is not about waiting for a title. It's about showing leadership qualities in the current role. Embracing the Four S's positions employees as indispensable contributors and prepares them for the next step in their careers.

APPLICATION: TURNING INSIGHT INTO PRACTICE

The Four S's—Strategy, Synergy, Systems, and Stories—are only as powerful as the actions they inspire. To bring these concepts to life, organizations must focus on practical shifts in behavior, decision-making, and culture that align with this framework. These changes don't require sweeping overhauls but rather intentional adjustments that ripple through teams and processes, creating meaningful impact.

Behavior Shifts

Leaders and employees alike can begin by adopting a mindset of the Four S's. Leaders should actively create space for others to step into decision-making roles, encouraging team members to take initiative and solve problems without waiting for direction. Employees, in turn, can focus on showing leadership in their current roles by identifying opportunities for improvement, collaborating across teams, and following through on commitments. These small, consistent actions build trust and credibility, fostering a culture where leadership is distributed rather than concentrated.

Decision-Making Changes

Decision-making becomes more intentional when guided by the Four S's. Leaders can use strategy as a filter for prioritizing initiatives, asking, "Does this align with our long-term vision?" Synergy encourages decisions that involve collaboration, ensuring that diverse perspectives are considered before moving forward. Systems provide clarity by standardizing processes, making it easier to delegate decisions to those closest to the action. Stories, meanwhile, remind decision-makers to consider the human impact of their choices, ensuring that decisions resonate with both employees and customers.

Organizational Implications

At an organizational level, the Four S's create a foundation for sustainable growth and resilience. Strategy ensures that resources are allocated effectively, reducing wasted effort and aligning teams around shared goals. Synergy breaks down silos, fostering a culture of collaboration that drives innovation and problem-solving. Systems create consistency and scalability, enabling the organization to adapt to change without losing its core values. Stories humanize the brand, building trust and loyalty among employees and customers alike.

These shifts don't require perfection; they require progress. Organizations that embrace the Four S's as a guiding framework will find that small, intentional changes lead to significant results over time. Leadership becomes more distributed, teams become more aligned, and the organization becomes more adaptable, creating a thriving environment where both people and the business can flourish.

PUTTING OWNERSHIP INTO PRACTICE

The Four S's—Synergy, Systems, Strategy, and Structure—create the foundation for a culture where ownership thrives. Leaders strengthen Synergy by fostering collaboration and shared accountability, while employees engage with Systems to drive meaningful improvements within established workflows. Together, these efforts align with Strategy and are supported by Structure, turning ownership into action and innovation into impact.

Leader Action

Focus on reinforcing Synergy by identifying one cross-functional project or task that could benefit from collaboration. Pair team members from different departments or roles and give them the space to work together, solve problems, and take ownership of the outcome. Provide a clear goal but allow them to determine the best path forward, showing trust in their collective abilities.

Employee Action

Practice **Systems** by taking ownership of a process or workflow that could be improved. Identify inefficiencies or gaps, propose a solution, and take the lead in implementing it. Demonstrating initiative within an established structure shows leadership and builds credibility, even without formal authority.

Conversation Prompt

"Can you share a moment when your work made a real impact on our larger goals? What tools or support would help you create more moments like that and take even greater ownership in shaping our success?"

This approach ties ownership directly to the Four S's. Leaders foster **Synergy** by encouraging collaboration and shared accountability, while employees engage with **Systems** to create meaningful improvements. The conversation prompt connects individual contributions to the broader **Strategy**, reinforcing alignment and purpose. Together, these actions and dialogues build a culture where ownership thrives, supported by the Four S's framework.

When the Four S's lay the foundation, entrepreneurial behavior becomes the driving force that turns structure into innovation and ownership into action.

PART THREE
DEVELOPING LEADERS BEFORE THEY LEAD

5
SPOTTING ENTREPRENEURIAL THINKING

"Some people are born with a builder's spirit—they treat every challenge as a chance to create something lasting, act as if the future rests in their hands, and see opportunities for growth in places others overlook." —Jamie Anne Gustafson

One of the greatest feelings I had when I started my own business was finally wearing the title of "entrepreneur." It wasn't just a label —it felt like a perfect fit for who I was. I had always been the person who saw opportunity where others saw roadblocks, who thought outside the box, and who constantly pushed for better ways to do things. It was an identity that made sense of my restless energy.

When I eventually sold my business and transitioned to another firm, the hardest part wasn't the workflow change—it was losing that sense of identity. I hated feeling like I had left that part of myself behind at the closing table. Yet, as I settled into new roles, I realized something profound—I was still playing that role. It didn't matter what title was printed on my name tag or employment contract. Whether I was waiting tables, pulling espresso shots as a barista, serving as an airman, or managing a busy office, I was still looking for ways to innovate and improve.

I realized then that this type of thinking wasn't a job description; it was a gift. It is a mindset that transcends hierarchy. For any organization, finding someone with this innate entrepreneurial spirit is like striking gold and signals a clear need to cultivate a leadership development path for that individual. The challenge, however, lies in identification. In a sea of employees doing their jobs, how do you distinguish the ones who are truly thinking like owners?

We use a simple framework to cut through the noise and spot this mindset—Inquiry, Communication, and Resolution. Inquiry kicks in when someone refuses to accept the status quo and questions why things are the way they are, diving deeper than the surface level. Communication shines through when a person effectively shares their ideas, collaborates with others, and ensures everyone is aligned. Finally, Resolution shows up when someone takes decisive action to implement those ideas and solve challenges, even when the path forward is uncertain.

WHY THIS MATTERS

When team members step up, spot challenges, and implement creative solutions, they not only resolve immediate problems but also spark momentum and drive collective progress. Fostering this mindset across all levels of an organization strengthens leadership skills, builds trust, and encourages a culture where everyone feels responsible for success. This is what makes companies more adaptive, resilient, and healthy in the long run. The ability to recognize entrepreneurial thinking on your team is vital for organizational growth. These moments of initiative and creativity don't happen only in corner offices. They occur on the front lines, in support roles, and everywhere in between. Spotting these behaviors early fosters not just individual growth but a culture of ownership that can transform your organization's trajectory.

CORE CONCEPT & FRAMEWORK

At its heart, entrepreneurial thinking is about the everyday choices people make when facing a challenge. Maybe it is a barista who reimagines the morning rush, a team member who proposes a smarter way forward, or anyone who sees a roadblock and asks, "What can we do differently, right now?"

We use a simple framework to cut through the noise and spot this mindset: Inquiry, Communication, and Resolution. Inquiry kicks in when someone refuses to accept the status quo and questions why things are the way they are, diving deeper than the surface level.

Communication shines through when a person effectively shares their ideas, collaborates with others, and ensures everyone is aligned. Finally, Resolution shows up when someone takes decisive action to implement those ideas and solve challenges, even when the path forward is uncertain.

When you start looking for Inquiry, Communication, and Resolution, no matter where you are in the organization, you'll spot the spark that leads to ownership and growth. That's how cultures shift, one bold idea at a time.

BREWING LEADERSHIP: HOW ENTREPRENEURIAL THINKING TRANSFORMS TEAMS

Sara glanced over the crowded coffee shop, feeling tension ripple through the staff as the Monday morning rush grew. The line of customers snaked out the door, and frustration simmered both behind the counter and in the lobby. Regulars tapped their feet impatiently. Baristas hustled to keep up, but with only one register running and a backlog of online orders, the flow had ground to a near halt. Management's solution was always to "just push through," but it never really worked.

Sara studied the scene, seeking a solution rather than succumbing to the chaos. She quickly called over two teammates, suggesting they open the usually idle second counter, a move typically saved for mid-morning lulls. While her colleagues hesitated, she confidently reassigned one barista to the register and another to handle drinks. Almost immediately, the team felt relief as some of the pressure lifted and a second line began to form.

Noticing that the mobile order shelf was cluttered with to-go cups awaiting pickup, Sara realized this was slowing everyone down. She rolled a table closer to the entrance and moved all the finished online orders there, clearly labeling pick-up spots for easy access. This freed up precious counter space and let the baristas focus on making drinks, rather than fielding questions about missing orders.

As her teammates adapted to the new setup, the lines moved faster, and confusion melted away. Customers started chatting and smiling again instead of glancing at their watches. The staff found their rhythm, working more smoothly and with renewed energy now that the bottleneck had been cleared. Instead of waiting for management or hoping the rush would die down, Sara spotted the opportunity to make things better and acted decisively. Her initiative not only ensured a smooth morning but also provided both coworkers and customers with a much-needed sense of calm and order amid chaos.

Sara's willingness to step forward didn't just solve the problem— it reignited her team's morale and built a ripple effect of ownership. Others began sharing observations and suggestions, helping prevent future issues. Sara, refusing to accept the lull and looking for opportunities instead, demonstrated that entrepreneurial thinking can emerge anywhere and that recognizing and supporting this mindset can unlock growth for everyone. The ability to recognize entrepreneurial thinking on your team is vital for organizational growth. These moments of initiative and creativity don't only happen in corner offices. They occur on front lines, in support roles, and everywhere in between. Spotting these behaviors early fosters not just individual growth but a culture of ownership that can transform your organization's trajectory.

Sometimes, the spark of curiosity is what gets things moving. Then creativity finds a fresh approach, and courage follows through with action, three simple traits that define entrepreneurial thinking. Sara's story is a reminder that you don't have to be in charge or have a fancy title to make things better. Still, you need to be willing to notice what others overlook, imagine a solution, and act, even if it means coloring a bit outside the lines.

Every workplace has people like Sara, those who inquire, communicate, and resolve. A leader's real job is to notice these moments, reward questions instead of brushing them aside, make room for safe experiments, and recognize the courage it takes to go first. Spotting and supporting these behaviors means you're nurturing your team's greatest asset: the drive to make things better, no matter where you start.

Spotting entrepreneurial thinking does more than create one-off improvements. It actively builds strategic leaders at every level, those who demonstrate initiative, an eye for opportunity, and the persistence to drive meaningful change. When you encourage Inquiry, you develop people who seek to understand the bigger picture, question the status quo, and ask the right questions. When an organization values Communication, it fosters collaboration, ensures alignment, and empowers individuals to share ideas effectively. When Resolution is prioritized, you inspire decisive action to implement solutions and overcome challenges, even when the outcome is uncertain.

Together, these traits prepare people to lead, whether they're running a shift or steering a department. They become the ones who see around corners, connect dots others miss, and inspire those around them to do the same. This willingness to take ownership and shape outcomes, regardless of title, is the foundation of lasting organizational health and success. Nurturing these qualities ensures that leadership is not confined to the top but grows everywhere talent and drive are found.

DUAL WIFM LENSES (WHAT'S IN IT FOR ME?)

Fostering agency within your team transforms leadership from reactive problem-solving to proactive talent cultivation. Empowered team members who take ownership of their actions and decisions create a ripple effect, reducing the need for constant oversight and enabling leaders to focus on strategy and growth. This shift builds a culture of curiosity, creativity, and courage, where entrepreneurial thinking thrives and drives long-term success.

Leader Lens: Why This Matters Upstream

For leaders and managers, understanding and fostering agency, the sense of ownership over one's actions and decisions within your team, is transformative. Entrepreneurial thinking becomes more than a buzzword when team members feel empowered to influence outcomes. It shifts your role from being the primary problem-solver to that of a talent cultivator with agency. Instead of merely directing tasks, your focus shifts to creating an environment in which curiosity, creativity, and courage can flourish at all levels. This change means you spend less time managing crises and more time empowering your team to prevent them. It's a move from transactional management to strategic leadership, where active agency fuels proactive engagement.

When agency and entrepreneurial thinking are present, leaders build teams that examine challenges in layers, exploring not only what's visible but also the underlying systems and patterns. Team members empowered with agency are more likely to question, probe, and propose creative alternatives, expanding the range of possible solutions. This habit of thinking beyond what's immediately in front of them leads to more robust strategies that anticipate roadblocks, yielding smarter decisions for the future.

Leaders who deliberately use the framework of Inquiry, Communication, and Resolution gain a practical pathway to be intentional about leadership development and nurture agency across all roles. Rather than relying on outdated or rigid advancement models, you can focus on spotting and developing these core traits that fuel agency. Encouraging Inquiry helps team members ask the right questions, challenge the status quo, and seek deeper understanding. Prioritizing Communication fosters collaboration, alignment, and the effective exchange of ideas. Emphasizing Resolution inspires decisive action, empowering individuals to implement solutions and effect meaningful change.

This approach helps address common leadership pipeline issues by nurturing the mindsets and behaviors required for effective leadership, rather than waiting for a title or position to be granted.

Embracing agency directly impacts development, retention, and decision-making. When you actively look for and reward entrepreneurial behaviors, you send a clear signal that initiative and ownership are valued at every level. Employees who feel their agency is recognized are more likely to stay engaged and committed. This approach decentralizes decision-making, enabling quicker, more informed choices by those closest to the problem. Your organization becomes more agile and resilient as agency turns intent into action throughout the team.

Leaders should begin to recognize the quiet innovators and proactive problem-solvers who may lack formal authority but demonstrate clear ownership and agency. Your role is to do more than acknowledge their efforts. It's to actively clear roadblocks so their agency and ideas can flourish. Ask your team what would happen if they tried a different approach. Celebrate the learning that comes from a failed experiment. Your deliberate actions to foster a culture of agency will turn passive employees into active partners in the company's success.

Employee Lens: Why This Matters on the Ground

For employees, developing agency through an entrepreneurial mindset is the key to unlocking credibility and influence, regardless of your job title. Agency means you believe your actions can change outcomes, and you make choices accordingly. When you consistently demonstrate curiosity and a drive to find better solutions, you build a reputation as someone who adds value beyond your core responsibilities. Your colleagues and managers begin to see you as a go-to person for tough challenges, which naturally elevates your standing and gives your voice more weight in important conversations.

Those who think entrepreneurially harness agency to see their work through multiple lenses, considering not just the obvious fix but also alternate approaches and hidden opportunities others may miss. Problem-solving shifts from linear to layered, with employees exploring different angles, uncovering root causes, and connecting solutions across departments. This ownership and sense of agency unlock greater trust and influence because leadership recognizes the rare quality of a broad, strategic perspective.

This approach demonstrates true ownership and agency long before formal authority. Authority is given, but agency and ownership are claimed. These show up when you treat company resources like your own, when you take the initiative to fix a broken process instead of complaining, and when you collaborate to solve a problem that isn't technically yours to tackle. These actions make it clear that you are invested in the outcome, not the task, marking you as a leader in practice, not in title.

Consistent practice of Inquiry, Communication, and Resolution strengthens agency and prepares you for leadership roles. Engaging in Inquiry trains you to ask insightful questions, uncover complexity, and challenge the status quo with confidence. Practicing Communication helps you share ideas effectively, collaborate with others, and align teams toward a common goal. Embracing Resolution empowers you to take decisive action, even on a small scale, building confidence in your decision-making and agency in your own growth trajectory. These behaviors help you look beyond the obvious and operate with a leader's mindset— because agency starts with believing you can make a difference, no matter where you are in the organization.

APPLICATION: TURNING INSIGHT INTO PRACTICE

Insights are valuable, but their true power is only realized when they're put into action. It's one thing to identify an opportunity for growth or a new way of thinking. However, it's something else entirely to turn that knowledge into tangible results. The gap between understanding and action is bridged by practical steps that gradually reshape how people behave, make decisions, and participate in the organization's culture.

Imagine a team curious about how to foster innovative thinking. Instead of leaders issuing top-down mandates, small, intentional actions begin to shift the day-to-day rhythm. People start sharing ideas at team meetings, and maybe the first few minutes are set aside specifically for creative brainstorming. One person sketches out a process improvement and shares it with others. Managers take note, not just by giving lip service, but by celebrating these actions publicly, especially when someone dares to question long-standing, but inefficient processes. This visibility encourages more people to try.

Trying something new always comes with risk, so the organization intentionally makes it safe to experiment. Departments run low-stakes pilot programs, such as tweaking a workflow or allowing someone to spend part of their time on a new project. As these experiments unfold, the fear of messing up fades, and soon, participation grows. Leaders and peers alike learn that it's not the flawless result that matters most, but the courage to propose, test, and learn from new ideas. Even when things don't work out, people are recognized for the act of trying, and this builds a culture where stepping outside comfort zones becomes second nature.

Once the seeds of new behaviors are planted, their impact extends to decision-making. Rather than relying on traditional top-down authority, power shifts outward. Those closest to a challenge are trusted to solve it, supported with resources and trust from their managers. A customer service representative, for instance, might be empowered to resolve issues without waiting for approval from above, provided they document what happened. Decision-making becomes more agile, evidence-based, and faster because teams are encouraged to ask, "What information led us here?" Instead of arguments resting on personal opinions, ideas are supported by data, curiosity, and thoughtful analysis.

The organization improves at distinguishing between major irreversible decisions that require care and "two-way doors" that can be quickly tried and reversed if needed. As these reversible choices are made at a faster pace, the company becomes increasingly adaptive, learning through rapid feedback instead of lengthy debate.

These shifts aren't isolated. They ripple through the organization, reshaping culture and expectations. Leaders view their role differently, moving away from gatekeeping toward cultivating the conditions for growth. They work to clear obstacles, ensure teams have what they need, and serve as buffers while teams experiment bravely. When the team succeeds, leaders celebrate alongside them. But, when failure happens, leaders absorb the fallout, reinforcing psychological safety so no one is afraid to try again.

Recognition becomes key. The organization's values are spelled out not in memos but in who and what it rewards. Innovators are called out, spot bonuses might go to those who tackle tough problems, and stories of initiative are told. This visible appreciation ensures everyone sees that taking ownership, before it's even formally granted, matters deeply.

At its core, this journey is about embracing continuous learning. Formal and informal spaces pop up for sharing knowledge, maybe in a post-project review or during a casual lunch-and-learn. Digital spaces archive insights and lessons learned. As people, teams, and leaders adapt to new information, their ability to put insight into action becomes a lasting advantage, one rooted in curiosity, courage, and the collective drive to shape the future.

PUTTING OWNERSHIP INTO PRACTICE

Entrepreneurial thinking is the spark that transforms contributors into catalysts for organizational change. Leaders play a pivotal role in identifying and nurturing team members who demonstrate Inquiry, Communication, and Resolution that challenge the status quo. This intentional focus not only fosters a culture of ownership but also signals that proactive, solution-oriented behavior is essential for leadership development and long-term success.

Leader Action

Identify one team member who has recently demonstrated initiative or creative problem-solving, and schedule a one-on-one conversation with them. During the discussion, acknowledge their efforts, ask what motivated their approach, and explore how their skills could be applied to larger challenges or opportunities within the organization. This not only reinforces their entrepreneurial mindset but also signals your commitment to recognizing and fostering ownership.

Employee Action

The next time you notice an issue or obstacle, pause before jumping straight into a quick fix. Ask yourself if there could be a deeper cause beneath the obvious problem. Take a moment to "peel the onion" by examining why the issue keeps coming up, or if there's a broader process or pattern that needs attention. When you think beyond the immediate symptom, you may uncover a root cause and help shape a more lasting, effective solution. Furthermore, you will find areas that present opportunities for the company.

Conversation Prompt

Encourage a deeper conversation by practicing the art of asking why. The next time you discuss a recurring challenge or unexpected result, take turns asking "why" up to five times to get beyond the surface and uncover root causes. For example:

- "Why did this (name the gap) issue occur?"
- "Why do we think that (name the gap) happened?"
- "Why does our process make that (name the gap) possible?"
- Continue until you both feel you've reached the underlying cause.

In chapter three of this book, the importance of naming the gap when addressing frustrations was discussed. To avoid assigning blame with 'why' questions, focus on highlighting the specific issue at hand rather than the person involved. This approach creates a safe space for curiosity, helps you both see the bigger picture, and often reveals actionable solutions that a quick fix might miss.

Once you have addressed the gap at hand, it is essential to work with the employee on intentional growth by asking, "What is one thing in your role that you feel you have complete ownership over, and what is one area where you wish you had more influence or autonomy?"

This question achieves two critical goals. First, it helps you understand the employee's current perception of their own agency and impact. Second, it facilitates a collaborative discussion about where you can remove barriers or provide additional support. The conversation moves from what the employee is *doing* to how they can contribute more meaningfully, reinforcing buy-in on both sides.

Once entrepreneurial thinking shifts from a sporadic trait to a daily habit, the employee ceases to be just a contributor and becomes a catalyst for broader organizational change.

6

FROM CONTRIBUTOR
TO CATALYST

"Organizational leadership formation emerges when ownership becomes habitual—where taking initiative, inspiring action, and creating lasting impact is woven into the fabric of daily work." — Jamie Anne Gustafson

The day Patrick joined the team, I could tell he was eager to make an impact. Coming from a corporate background, he was used to structure, clear processes, defined roles, and a roadmap to follow. However, this role was different. We had hired him to help take our e-card division to the next level, a product line we were expanding but hadn't yet fully defined. There was no playbook, no established process, just a vision and a room full of potential.

To ease him in, I started Patrick with a smaller project, something manageable that wouldn't disrupt the larger operation if it didn't go as planned. Over coffee one morning, we brainstormed ideas. Patrick was brimming with energy, throwing out concepts and solutions I hadn't considered before. Some of his ideas felt unconventional, even risky, and I wasn't entirely sure they would work. But I could see his enthusiasm and the logic behind his thinking, so I decided to give him the space to explore.

"Let's start small," I said, "and see where this takes us."

Patrick dove in, and within a week, he came back with a solution that was not only logical but surprisingly innovative. It streamlined the process in ways I hadn't anticipated. I was impressed but cautious. "This is great," I told him, "but do you think this could work on a bigger scale?"

He didn't hesitate. "I don't see why not," he said confidently.

That was the moment I realized I needed to step back and let Patrick take the reins. Even though I wasn't entirely sure of the outcome, I trusted his process and allowed him to execute his ideas. What happened next was nothing short of transformative. The solution Patrick implemented didn't just work—it opened a whole new world of possibilities for the e-card division. His approach revealed applications we hadn't even considered, and the ripple effect was felt across the entire team.

Before long, Patrick wasn't only managing small projects but he was leading the entire division. His ability to think strategically, take ownership, and execute with confidence had turned a fledgling product line into a thriving part of our business. Watching him grow into his role was a powerful reminder of what happens when you give people the space to experiment, trust their instincts, and take ownership of their work.

Patrick's journey wasn't just about his success. It was about the culture we created together. By giving him the freedom to explore and the support to take risks, we unlocked not only his potential but the potential of the entire division. It was a lesson in leadership I'll never forget. Sometimes, the best thing you can do as a leader is step back, trust your team, and let them surprise you.

WHY THIS MATTERS

Patrick's story highlights the transformative power of ownership in leadership development and organizational health. When individuals are given the space to experiment, take risks, and own their work, they unlock creativity and innovation that can advance entire divisions. For leaders, this means shifting from micromanagement to trust, allowing team members to realize their potential, even when the path is uncertain.

Ownership fosters confidence, strategic thinking, and accountability, which are the building blocks of leadership. For organizations, this approach creates a culture where people feel empowered to contribute beyond their roles, leading to stronger teams, better solutions, and long-term growth. Leadership isn't about having all the answers; it's about creating an environment where others can find them.

CORE CONCEPT & FRAMEWORK

The journey from contributor to catalyst begins with ownership. Leadership isn't about titles or authority—it's a behavior that emerges when individuals take initiative, think strategically, and act with purpose. This transformation is captured in the **Contributor to Catalyst Model**, which highlights four key stages: **ownership**, where individuals take responsibility for outcomes rather than just tasks; **initiative**, where they proactively solve problems and make decisions; **influence**, where consistent action builds credibility and inspires others; and **impact**, where they shift from simply completing work to shaping outcomes that drive organizational success. Leadership formation, rather than accidental methods, ensures this growth is intentional, creating an environment where ownership becomes habitual, and leaders are developed at every level, fostering a culture of resilience, innovation, and long-term success.

FROM CONTRIBUTOR TO CATALYST: BUILDING LEADERS THROUGH INTENTIONAL SYSTEMS

When new employees join an established division, it's easy for them to slip into the role of a passenger, following the processes, doing the tasks, and staying within the lines. But I've learned that if we want to develop leaders, we can't let them stay in the passenger seat for long. Leadership formation requires intentionality, a system that moves people from simply contributing to becoming catalysts for growth and innovation.

In my approach, new employees start by riding shotgun. They observe, learn the systems, and get a feel for how the division operates. This is their time to absorb the culture, understand the expectations, and see how the team works together. But this phase doesn't last forever. Once they've gained their footing, they're handed the keys.

When it's their turn to drive, they're given real responsibility, but with feedback and oversight. I don't just throw them into the deep end and hope for the best. Instead, I stay close, offering guidance and asking questions to help them think critically about their decisions. This phase is about building confidence and competence, giving them the space to take ownership while knowing they have a safety net.

The process doesn't stop there. After they've had time to drive, I turn the tables and ask for their feedback. "What worked for you? What didn't? How can we make this process better?" These conversations are critical because they shift the focus from simply following the system to improving it. New employees bring fresh perspectives, and their insights often lead to innovations that make the entire division stronger.

One of the most powerful tools I've found for leadership formation is the concept of job creation. I ask every team member, "What makes you shine? What parts of your role energize you, and what parts weigh you down?" These questions aren't just about making their jobs more enjoyable. They're about uncovering their unique strengths and aligning them with the needs of the organization.

I also ask, "Where do you see opportunity for yourself and for the company?" This question shifts their mindset from task-oriented to future-focused. It encourages them to think strategically about their role, their potential, and how they can contribute to the company's growth.

These conversations are transformative. They help employees see themselves not just as contributors, but as catalysts—people who drive change, solve problems, and create value. They also help me, as a leader, identify opportunities to align individuals' strengths with the company's goals, creating a mutually beneficial situation that benefits both the individual and the organization.

The Contributor to Catalyst Model in Action

This approach reflects the **Contributor to Catalyst Model**, a powerful framework that outlines the stages of leadership development. It begins with **Ownership**, the foundational stage in which new employees assume responsibility for their roles. At this stage, they focus on learning the systems, understanding expectations, and gradually stepping into the driver's seat. Ownership is about more than just completing tasks—it's about taking accountability for outcomes and beginning to see how their work fits into the bigger picture. This stage lays the groundwork for deeper engagement and sets the tone for their journey toward leadership.

As employees gain confidence and competence, they progress to the stage of **Initiative**. Here, they are encouraged to think critically, identify opportunities for improvement, and solve problems proactively. Initiative is the practice of employees moving beyond the boundaries of their job descriptions, offering ideas and taking action to enhance processes, projects, or outcomes. This stage is critical because it fosters creativity and a sense of agency, empowering employees to view themselves as contributors to the organization's success rather than merely as task executors.

From initiative comes **Influence**, a stage where employees' actions and insights begin to inspire those around them. Influence is not tied to formal authority—it's about earning trust and respect through consistent performance, innovative thinking, and a collaborative mindset. Employees at this stage contribute to a culture of innovation and shared accountability, encouraging their peers to step up and take ownership as well. Influence is where leadership begins to emerge organically, as individuals demonstrate their ability to guide, motivate, and elevate others.

The final stage is **Impact**, where employees move beyond simply completing tasks to actively shaping outcomes that drive the company forward. At this stage, they are not participants in the organization—they are catalysts for growth and change. They adopt a strategic view of their work, aligning their efforts with the company's goals and creating meaningful, lasting value. Impact is the culmination of the Contributor-to-Catalyst journey, in which individuals fully embrace their role as leaders, regardless of their title or position.

This model is not a rigid, linear path but a dynamic and iterative process. Employees may move back and forth between stages as they encounter new challenges, take on different roles, or face setbacks. For leaders, the key is to guide this progression thoughtfully, creating an environment where ownership, initiative, influence, and impact can thrive. When organizations foster this journey, they don't just develop individual leaders—they build a culture of leadership that drives innovation, resilience, and long-term success.

Leadership formation isn't accidental; it's intentional. When creating systems that guide employees from observation to ownership, and by leading with the concept of job creation, we develop leaders who are not only contributors but catalysts for growth. This approach doesn't just benefit the individual. It strengthens the entire organization, creating a culture of resilience, innovation, and long-term success.

When employees are given the tools, the space, and the encouragement to shine, they don't just do their jobs—they transform them. In doing so, they transform the company. That's the power of intentional leadership formation, and it's how we turn contributors into catalysts.

DUAL WIFM LENSES (WHAT'S IN IT FOR ME?)

When employees feel empowered to take initiative and solve problems, their contributions go beyond completing assignments— they actively shape outcomes and drive progress. This shift allows leaders to focus on strategy and long-term goals, knowing their teams are fully engaged in creating value at every level.

Leader Lens: Why This Matters Upstream

For leaders and managers, this approach transforms how talent is developed and retained. By fostering ownership, leaders create a culture in which employees not only complete tasks but also actively contribute to the organization's success. This shift reduces turnover, as employees who feel empowered and valued are more likely to stay and grow within the company.

It also enhances decision-making. When employees take ownership, they bring fresh ideas and solutions to the table, giving leaders a broader perspective and better insights. This collaborative dynamic ensures that decisions are informed by those closest to the work, leading to more effective and innovative outcomes.

Leaders should pay attention to how their teams respond to opportunities for ownership. Are employees stepping up with ideas? Are they taking initiative? If not, it's a signal to adjust the environment, perhaps by providing clearer expectations, asking for input, or creating more space for experimentation. Leaders who prioritize ownership will see stronger engagement, better performance, and a more resilient team.

This approach also shifts the leader's role from sole decision-maker to coach and enabler. When the organization focuses on creating systems that encourage ownership, leaders are free to focus on strategy and long-term vision while empowering their teams to handle the day-to-day challenges.

Employee Lens: Why This Matters on the Ground

For employees, ownership is the key to unlocking credibility, confidence, and influence. When you take responsibility for outcomes-not just tasks—you demonstrate reliability and initiative, which builds trust with your peers and managers. This trust is the foundation of leadership, even before you hold a formal title.

Ownership also builds confidence. When you're given the space to solve problems, make decisions, and take risks, you develop the skills and self-assurance needed to lead. Each success reinforces your ability to handle greater challenges, preparing you for future opportunities.

Leadership often begins long before authority is granted. Behaviors like proactively identifying solutions, offering constructive feedback, and seeking ways to improve processes show that you're thinking strategically and acting with the organization's success in mind. These actions set you apart as someone ready to lead.

This approach also helps employees align their strengths with their roles. Reflecting on what energizes you and where you see growth opportunities, you can shape your job into something that not only benefits the company but also allows you to shine. Leadership isn't about waiting for a title; it's about showing up every day with ownership, initiative, and a commitment to making an impact.

APPLICATION: TURNING INSIGHT INTO PRACTICE

Shifting from contributor to catalyst requires intentional behavior changes at every level of the organization. For leaders, this means creating an environment where ownership is encouraged and supported. Instead of solving every problem or dictating every step, leaders can focus on asking better questions— "What do you think? How would you approach this?" This small shift in behavior empowers employees to think critically and take initiative, fostering a culture of problem-solving and innovation.

Decision-making also evolves. Leaders who embrace this approach move from being the sole decision-makers to facilitators of decisions. By involving employees in the process and valuing their input, leaders gain access to diverse perspectives and ideas. This not only improves the quality of decisions but also increases buy-in and accountability across the team. Employees, in turn, learn to weigh options, consider trade-offs, and make decisions with confidence—skills that prepare them for leadership roles.

At an organizational level, this approach has far-reaching implications. When ownership becomes a core value, it creates a ripple effect. Teams become more engaged, proactive, and resilient. Processes improve as employees feel empowered to identify inefficiencies and propose solutions. Retention rates increase when individuals perceive opportunities for growth and feel their contributions are valued.

The key is to embed these shifts into daily practices. Leaders can create space for reflection by holding regular debriefs after projects, asking what worked, what didn't, and what could be improved. Employees can be encouraged to align their strengths with their roles by reflecting on what energizes them and where they see growth opportunities. These practices turn insight into action, ensuring that leadership formation becomes a natural part of how the organization operates.

Ultimately, this approach isn't about overhauling systems overnight —it's about small, intentional changes that build momentum over time. By focusing on ownership, decision-making, and alignment, organizations can create a culture where leadership emerges at every level, driving innovation, resilience, and long-term success.

PUTTING OWNERSHIP INTO PRACTICE

Ownership is a journey shaped by experiences, opportunities, and intentional guidance.

Leader Action

Reevaluate your onboarding process with leadership formation in mind. Identify one way to integrate opportunities for ownership early on—whether it's assigning a small project where the new hire can take the lead or creating a structured "ride shotgun, then drive" approach. Build in moments for feedback and reflection to help them connect their actions to the bigger picture.

Employee Action

Take a moment to write your "perfect job description." Think about the tasks and responsibilities that energize you, the areas where you feel you could make the biggest impact, and the skills you'd like to develop further. Use this guide to identify areas in your current role where you can lean in and take greater ownership.

Conversation Prompt

"If you were to design your perfect job description, what would it look like? How can we align your strengths and interests with opportunities to grow in your role?"

This approach encourages employees to take an active role in shaping their contributions while giving leaders valuable insights into how to support and develop their teams. It's a powerful way to build ownership and leadership formation into the foundation of every role.

Leadership isn't a destination—it's a journey. It's a developmental process that unfolds over time, shaped by experiences, opportunities, and intentional guidance. Ownership, at its core, is the bridge between where someone is today and where they have the potential to go. But this journey isn't a straight line. It's a dynamic, non-linear process that requires reinforcement, reflection, and adaptability at every stage.

In Chapter 7, we'll explore the **5-Stage Ownership Journey**, a framework that maps out how individuals grow from contributors to catalysts. These stages aren't rigid steps to be climbed in order, but rather a fluid progression that reflects the realities of personal and professional growth. Each stage builds on the last, but setbacks, plateaus, and moments of recalibration are all part of the process.

For leaders, the role isn't to force progression or push people through the stages. Instead, it's about creating the conditions for growth, offering guidance, and recognizing when to step back and let individuals take the lead. Leadership in this context is about being a coach, a mentor, and a partner in the journey—not a dictator of outcomes.

PART FOUR
THE OWNERSHIP JOURNEY

7
THE 5-STAGE OWNERSHIP JOURNEY

STAGE 1: AWARENESS: SEE THE BIGGER PICTURE

"People can't soar if they're tethered to the ground—give them the room to fly, and they'll discover heights you never imagined." —
Jamie Anne Gustafson

The Disconnected Cog

In a small but beloved artisan bakery, the team prided itself on one thing above all—quality. Every loaf of bread was made with care, using the finest ingredients and time-honored techniques. Customers raved about the bakery's rich sourdough, flaky croissants, and perfectly balanced pastries. It wasn't just food; it was an experience.

However, the bakery's social media marketer, Emma, had a different focus. She was determined to drive sales, so her posts featured flashy discounts, "Buy One Get One" deals, and constant reminders to "Order Now!" While the promotions brought in some short-term traffic, they didn't reflect what made the bakery special.

Emma was missing the bigger picture. The bakery's **strength** wasn't in being the cheapest or most accessible option. It was in its unmatched quality and craftsmanship. Customers weren't coming for a deal, they were coming for the best bread in town. By focusing on quick sales tactics, Emma overlooked the opportunity to build a brand that celebrated the bakery's artistry, story, and connection to the community.

Emma wasn't failing because she wasn't working hard. She was just rowing in the wrong direction. She didn't see how leaning into the bakery's true strength could create a loyal following and long-term growth. Instead of amplifying what made the bakery unique, she was treating it like any other business, missing the chance to elevate it to something extraordinary.

Why This Matters

This is where leadership development often stalls before it even begins. We tend to throw new hires into the deep end of *tasks*. Here is your login, your desk, and your checklist. We mistakenly assume that if they do the tasks well enough for long enough, they will eventually absorb the "big picture" through osmosis.

They won't.

Awareness is the first critical step in the ownership journey. It is the transition from a passive employee who waits for instructions to an active participant who understands the ecosystem they inhabit. Without this stage, you get compliance, not commitment. You get employees who can follow a recipe but have no idea how to cook when an ingredient is missing.

Core Concept & Framework: The Awareness Audit

The mindset shift required here is profound but simple: **Employees don't just do work—they understand how work works.**

In Stage 1, we move away from the "need-to-know" basis of information sharing. Instead, we invite employees to conduct their own research. This isn't about memorizing a mission statement printed on a breakroom poster. It is about an active investigation into the engine of the organization.

The goal is to move the employee from asking, "What do I need to do today?" to asking, "How does what I do today help the company win?"

From Task-Taker to Value-Seeker

Let us go back to Emma and the bakery. The smell of freshly baked bread and buttery croissants fills the air, as it always has. The bakery is bustling, its loyal customers lining up for the sourdough loaves and pastries they've come to love. This small artisan bakery has always been known for its quality, its hallmark, its secret ingredient.

Emma, the bakery's social media marketer, is hard at work. But things are different now. Not long ago, Emma focused on driving sales with flashy discounts and urgent calls to action like "Order Now!" She thought that was the way to grow the business, to bring in more customers. However, her efforts weren't landing the way she'd hoped. The bakery's unique story, the one that had built its loyal following, was getting lost in the noise.

The owner noticed the disconnect. Emma was working hard, but her efforts weren't aligned with what made the bakery special. Instead of giving her another directive or lecture, the owner decided to take a different approach.

"Emma," she said, "I want you to take an hour this week to go through our customer reviews and find out why people love us. What keeps them coming back? Is it the price? Or is it something else?"

At first, Emma thought she already knew the answer: Who doesn't love a good deal? But as she began reading through the reviews, a different story started to emerge. Customers weren't raving about discounts or promotions. They discussed the taste, craftsmanship, and care that went into every loaf and pastry.

"This is the only place I'll buy bread—it tastes like it's made with love," one review said. Another read, "The croissants here remind me of the ones I had in Paris—worth every penny." Repeatedly, Emma saw the same themes—quality, authenticity, and the emotional connection customers felt to the bakery's products.

The owner didn't stop there. She invited Emma to spend time in the kitchen, shadowing the bakers. Emma watched as they carefully measured ingredients, kneaded dough by hand, and waited patiently for the perfect rise. She saw the pride they took in their work and the attention to detail that made every product exceptional.

It was a revelation. Emma realized that the bakery wasn't just selling bread, it was selling an experience, a story, a connection. Customers weren't coming for the lowest price—they were coming for the best quality and the feeling of indulgence and care that came with it.

This wasn't something Emma could have learned from another top-down directive. She had to discover it for herself. By taking the time to dig into the reviews and see the process up close, she replaced her assumptions with alignment. She understood the bakery's true value, and that understanding changed everything.

Emma completely transformed her marketing approach. She stopped focusing on discounts and started telling the bakery's story. She shared behind-the-scenes photos of the bakers at work, highlighted the premium ingredients used, and posted customer testimonials celebrating the product quality.

One post featured a video of a baker shaping dough, with the caption: "Every loaf of our sourdough is hand-crafted with care, using a 48-hour fermentation process for that perfect tangy flavor. Taste the difference." Another post showcased a customer review: "The croissants here are better than the ones I had in Paris—flaky, buttery perfection!"

The results were immediate. Customers began engaging with the bakery's social media in ways they never had before, commenting on how much they loved seeing the process and learning more about the products. Sales didn't just recover, they grew, as more people discovered the bakery and became loyal fans.

This shift didn't happen because Emma was told what to do. It happened because she was given the space to ask questions, to be curious, and to find the answers herself. The owner didn't broadcast the vision—they invited Emma to discover it.

This is the power of awareness. It replaces assumptions with alignment. When people understand the "why" behind their work, they don't need to be micromanaged or lectured. They change their behavior independently because they see the bigger picture.

For leaders, this means creating space for curiosity. It might feel counterintuitive to tell an employee to stop working for an hour to "think," but that hour can pay dividends in months of aligned effort. Emma's journey is proof of that. By taking the time to understand the bakery's true value, she didn't just become a better marketer. She became an advocate for the bakery's mission.

The bakery's story and Emma's transformation within it are a reminder that growth doesn't come from working harder or faster. It comes from working smarter, with a clear understanding of what makes your business special. Sometimes, the best way to find clarity is to stop, ask questions, and listen.

Dual WIFM Lenses (What's In It For Me?)

The Leader Lens

Why should you encourage your team to step away from execution to study the business? Because it stops you from being the bottleneck. When your team understands the "why" and the "how" of the business model, they stop asking you for permission on minor decisions. They know the destination so that they can navigate the route themselves. This frees you to focus on strategy rather than traffic control.

The Employee Lens

For you, the employee, this stage is about relevance. When you understand how the company makes money, who the customers are, and where the industry is headed, you stop being a replaceable cog. You become a partner. You gain the ability to spot opportunities that others miss because you aren't just looking at your desk, you're looking at the horizon.

Application: The "Perception Hour"

How do we turn this concept into practice? We stop spoon-feeding vision and start assigning discovery. In awareness, starting with strengths-first is best, as Emma found. What she thought was a weakness, the price, was actually not a weakness at all. Employees should employ a **Strengths-First Approach** before moving forward on any SWOT (Strengths, Weaknesses, Opportunities, and Threats) analysis.

For Leaders:

Instead of a standard onboarding presentation, assign your team members (new or existing) a "Perception Hour." Give them one hour a week for four weeks to research and answer four specific questions. Tell them there are no wrong answers, but you want to know how they see it.

The 4 Discovery Prompts:

- **How do we create value?** (Not just what do we sell, but why do people exchange money for it?)
- **What matters most to our customers?** (Is it speed, quality, price, relationship, or innovation?)
- **Where do decisions originate?** (Who decides what we build or sell, and what data do they use?)
- **What are we aiming to achieve?** (Beyond this quarter's revenue, what is the winning state for this company?)

For Employees:

Don't wait to be asked. Start your investigation. Look at the company's public filings, read customer reviews, assess competitors, and interview a colleague in a different department. Build your own mental map of the organization.

Putting Ownership into Practice

Awareness helps employees understand the company's influence on both customers and shareholders, fostering a broader sense of purpose. Applying a Strengths-First Approach to SWOT Analysis ensures that weaknesses and threats are considered in the context of the company's core strengths. Focusing on what sets the company apart allows employees to address challenges more effectively and approach potential risks with confidence.

Leader Action:

Schedule a review meeting after the "Perception Hour" exercises. Do not correct their findings immediately. Listen. If their perception is wrong, it means your communication channels are clogged. Use their answers as diagnostic data to improve how you share information. Use the four discovery prompts to start your Strengths-First SWOT Analysis. Then have the employee continue to learn more about the company's position as they progress through the analysis.

Employee Action:

Next time you are assigned a task, pause and ask yourself: "What value does this task bring to the customer or company? How does it lean into the strengths of the company?" If you can't answer it, go find out.

Conversation Prompt:

"Based on what you've seen this week, what is the one thing we do that adds the most value to our clients, and how does your role support that?"

Transition

Once an employee sees the bigger picture, they can no longer claim ignorance. They are now ready to move from understanding the map to finding their place upon it. Now, we must move from awareness to connection.

STAGE 2: ALIGNMENT: CONNECT YOUR ROLE TO THE MISSION

"Effort without alignment is just burnout waiting to happen. You can run fast, but if you're running in the wrong direction, you're just getting lost faster." —Jamie Anne Gustafson

When I first stepped into a leadership role, I believed success was about working hard, checking all the boxes, and delivering results. And I did just that. Yet, something still felt off. Despite my efforts, I wasn't truly connected to the bigger picture—or to the people around me. I was busy doing the work, but I wasn't driving the mission forward.

Then came a pivotal moment that changed everything. I was leading a team through a high-stakes project, and while everyone was putting in the effort, we weren't aligned. Each person was focused on their individual tasks, but those tasks weren't bringing us any closer to our shared goal. That's when it hit me—doing the job isn't enough. True success happens when we connect the doing to the driving. I realized I needed not only to find my own connection to the bigger picture but also to help my team see how their work fit into it. That's when everything began to shift.

Why This Matters

In Stage 1 (Awareness), we turned on the lights. Employees began to see the big picture. Now, in Stage 2, they must find their place within it.

Without alignment, you often get "disconnected excellence." This happens when talented people work hard on things that don't move the needle. They feel busy and productive, but the organization remains stagnant. This leads to frustration on both sides: leaders feel their goals aren't being met, and employees feel their hard work isn't being appreciated.

Alignment creates **relevance**. When an employee sees how their specific strengths and daily tasks contribute to the larger victory, engagement is no longer something you have to force. It becomes a natural byproduct of their work. Relevance is the foundation of buy-in.

Core Concept & Framework: The Three Pillars of Alignment

The mindset shift for Stage 2 is critical: **Employees are part of how this organization succeeds.**

It is not enough to simply "do" the job. You must connect the doing to the driving. To achieve this, we focus on three specific alignment points:

- **Strengths ↔ Business Needs:** Moving from "What am I good at?" to "How does what I'm good at solve a problem we actually have?"
- **Personal Goals ↔ Company Goals:** finding the intersection between where the individual wants to go

(career growth, skills) and where the company is going (market expansion, innovation).

- **Daily Effort ↔ Larger Vision:** Ensuring that the Tuesday morning to-do list actually supports the 5-year vision.

Finding the Intersection

Consider a customer support representative named David. He was naturally chatty and loved deep conversations. In a call center measured strictly by "Average Handle Time" (speed), David was failing. He was misaligned. He was using a strength (building rapport) in a system that valued speed.

Under traditional management, David would be put on a Performance Improvement Plan to talk less.

But a strategic leader looked for alignment. The company had a goal of increasing customer retention and reducing churn. The leader recognized David's "weakness" in speed as a significant strength for retention. They moved David to the "At-Risk Accounts" team, a role where long, empathetic conversations were the *goal*, not the problem.

David's performance skyrocketed. He didn't change who he was— he aligned his unique strength with the specific business need that valued it.

When employees align their personal strengths with business needs, friction disappears. Work stops feeling like a transaction ("I give you time, you give me money") and starts feeling like a contribution ("I give you talent, we achieve success").

Dual WIFM Lenses (What's In It For Me?)

The Leader Lens

Why invest time in alignment? Because aligned teams require less supervision. When your team understands the mission, you don't have to dictate every step. They can make autonomous decisions that support the goal because they know what the "win" looks like. It transforms you from a task manager to a momentum builder.

The Employee Lens

For you, alignment is the cure for burnout. Burnout often comes not from too much work, but from work that feels meaningless. When you align your personal goals with company goals, you aren't just building the CEO's dream. You are using the company as a vehicle to build your own career. You begin thinking about how to improve the company, not just how to perform your role well.

Application: The Alignment Audit

How do we move from theory to practice? We must map the connections.

For Leaders:

Stop hiring for generic "competence" and start looking for "mission match." For the team you already have, conduct an **Alignment Audit**.

- Look at your top three business goals for the year.
- Look at your employee's top three strengths.
- Ask: *Are these currently pointing at each other?*

If an employee is great at analysis but spends all day in meetings, they are misaligned. If they are great at people but stuck in spreadsheets, they are misaligned. Adjust the role to fit the mission.

For Employees:

You don't have to wait for a reorganization to align yourself. Perform a **Calendar Check**. Look at your tasks from last week. Highlight the ones that directly contributed to the company's top priorities in green. Highlight the ones that felt like "busy work" in red.

- If your week is mostly red, you are drifting.
- Ask yourself: *How can I use my strengths to turn more of this green?*

Putting Ownership into Practice

Effective leadership and teamwork happen when personal development connects with organizational objectives. Open conversations and proactive problem-solving help uncover new opportunities for success.

Leader Action:

In your next 1-on-1, ignore the status updates for ten minutes. Instead, ask about their personal goals. Ask, "What skills are you trying to build right now?" Then, look for a project on your plate that requires those skills and assign it to them. That is alignment, solving a business problem while fueling personal growth.

Employee Action:

Identify one friction point in your daily work that slows the team or frustrates customers. Propose a solution that uses your specific strengths to fix it. Don't ask, "What should I do?" Say, "I see this problem, and here is how I think I can help solve it."

Conversation Prompt:

"If you could rewrite your job description to focus 80% of your time on the things that drive the most value for our mission, what would you stop doing, and what would you do more of?"

Transition

Now that you see the big picture (Awareness) and have connected your role to the mission (Alignment), you are motivated to act. But motivation without method leads to chaos. You need the right tools to execute.

STAGE 3: APPLICATION: USE FRAMEWORKS TO CREATE VALUE

"Identifying a problem is common, but the ability to craft a solution with a clear view of the bigger picture is rare and invaluable." —Jamie Anne Gustafson

The Knowing-Doing Gap

We have all sat in that meeting. The one where a problem is identified, perhaps sales are down, or a software release is buggy, and the room descends into chaos. Opinions fly. Finger-pointing begins. People suggest random solutions based on what they did at their last job or what they read in a blog post that morning.

Everyone in the room is *aware* of the problem and the company's strength that can overcome it (Stage 1). Everyone is *aligned* on the desire to fix it (Stage 2). But they are failing to resolve it because they lack a shared approach to processing the solution. They are stuck in the "Knowing-Doing Gap."

In Stage 3, we bridge that gap. We move from the "what" and the "why" to the "how."

This stage is about **Application**. It is about applying the intellectual concepts of ownership in the real world. It is the shift from "I understand the vision" to "I am using a tool to execute the vision."

Why This Matters

Without frameworks, problem-solving is exhaustive and inconsistent. It relies entirely on the individual brilliance of a few people. If your "star player" is out sick, the problem doesn't get solved.

When you apply frameworks, you democratize high-level thinking. You give every employee a mental scaffold to hang their ideas on. This reduces anxiety because employees don't have to guess the right answer—they simply have to trust the process to reveal it.

Core Concept & Framework: Intentional Action

The Mindset Shift: **I understand. Now I act intentionally.**

In the previous chapters, we introduced several mental models. In this stage, we take them off the shelf. You aren't just "doing work" anymore; you are engineering value.

We apply the tools:

- **The Three F's (Failure, Frustration, Feedback):** Instead of getting emotional when things go wrong, you use this framework to extract data. You ask: *Is this a Failure of process? Is the Frustration a signal of friction? What does the Feedback tell us about the system?*
- **The Four S's:** You use this to diagnose organizational health. When a project stalls, you check the dials: *Is it a Strategy issue? A Synergy issue? A Systems issue? Or a Story issue?*
- **Spotting Entrepreneurial Thinking:** You actively filter your daily decisions through the lens of leverage. *Is this activity moving the needle, or just moving the papers?*
- **The Strengths-First SWOT Analysis:** You stop reserving this for annual retreats and start using it for Tuesday afternoon decisions. Internally, what strengths does the organization have, and how can it overcome any perceived weaknesses? Externally, what opportunities and threats are on the horizon?

The Meeting That Changed

Consider a marketing team at a retail chain. They were missing their Q3 targets. The weekly meeting was usually a grim affair of excuses: "The market is tough," "Competitors are discounting," "We don't have enough budget."

Then, a junior manager, Lakeesha, decided to apply a framework. Instead of offering an excuse, she walked to the whiteboard and drew a simple **Strengths-First Approach** as she mapped out the SWOT.

"Let's stop guessing," she said. "Let's map it."

She led the room through the grid. They realized their "Threat" (competitor discounting) was actually an "Opportunity" to pivot their messaging to quality, which was their identified "Strength."

When the company applied a framework, Lakeesha shifted the room from a helpless reaction to strategic action. She didn't have more authority than anyone else—she just had a better toolkit. The energy in the room changed instantly. They left with a plan, not a headache.

This is the essence of Stage 3: **You build confidence through execution.**

Dual WIFM Lenses (What's In It For Me?)

The Leader Lens

Why push frameworks? Because they create a common language. When your entire team uses the "Three F's" to discuss a mistake, you skip the blame game and go straight to the learning loop. Frameworks act as a neutral third party in the room, allowing you to critique the process without criticizing the person. This accelerates decision-making and reduces conflict.

The Employee Lens

For you, frameworks are confidence builders. When you face a complex problem that feels overwhelming, a framework provides a starting point. You don't have to be a genius; you just have to work the model. It turns vague anxiety into a concrete checklist. It makes you look—and feel—like the most organized thinker in the room.

Application: From Concept to Contribution

How do we start using these tools today?

For Leaders:

Stop accepting unstructured answers. When an employee brings you a problem, ask them, "Which framework are you using to analyze this?" If they are venting, guide them to the **Three F's**. If they are proposing a new idea, ask them to run it through a quick **4 S's**. Make the frameworks the "price of admission" for a decision-making meeting.

For Employees:

Pick one model to be your "Tool of the Week."

- **Week 1: The Three F's.** Every time you feel frustrated, write it down and analyze the root cause.
- **Week 2: The Four S's.** Look at a project that is stuck. Diagnose it. Is it the Strategy, Synergy, System, or Story?
- **Week 3: Entrepreneurial Thinking.** What is something that can be done to drive the business forward, not just maintain, but build?

Putting Ownership into Practice

Structured thinking has the power to transform how teams tackle challenges and make decisions. Replacing vague statements with insights grounded in proven frameworks fosters clarity and drives actionable solutions. Whether it's eliminating "I think" in retrospectives, analyzing blockages with the Four S's, or using Strength-First SWOT Analysis to break decision deadlocks, these practices encourage a culture of thoughtful, data-driven collaboration.

Leader Action:

In your next team retrospective, ban the phrase "I think." Challenge your team to frame their insights using one of the book's models. "Based on the 4 S's, I believe . . ." or "The Frustration points to a system failure in . . ."

Employee Action:

Before you send that email regarding a blocked project, apply a framework. Don't just report the blockage—report the analysis.

- *Bad:* "I can't finish this because IT is slow."
- *Good:* "I'm applying the **Four S's** here. We have a **System** bottleneck with IT. I propose we adjust our **Structure** to include a daily stand-up with them to clear blockers."

Conversation Prompt:

"We seem stuck on this decision. Let's pause and use the Strength-First SWOT Analysis process on the whiteboard for ten minutes to see if the data points us to a clear path. Who wants to hold the marker?"

Transition

You are now aware of the big picture, aligned with the mission, and applying the frameworks to create value. You are a contributor. But a true owner doesn't just contribute to the system—they improve it.

STAGE 4: INITIATIVE: IDENTIFY OPPORTUNITIES AND IMPROVE THE SYSTEM

"The difference between a worker and a leader is not a title. It is the ability to see a gap before an issue arises." —Jamie Anne Gustafson

The Silent Leak

At a busy logistics company, a manual data-entry process was widely disliked. It took each team member two hours every Friday to copy numbers from one spreadsheet to another. It was tedious, prone to error, and universally loathed.

For years, dozens of employees did it. They complained about it at lunch. They rolled their eyes when the calendar reminder popped up. Still, they did it because "that's just how we do things here."

Then came Julian. He had been with the company for only three months. He saw the process—he saw a **gap**. Instead of complaining, he spent his lunch break researching a simple macro script. He tested it on his own data. It worked.

The next Friday, he didn't just do his work; he sent an email to his manager: *"I noticed we spend about 20 collective hours a week on this report. I wrote a script that does it in 30 seconds. Here is the file and a quick video on how to use it."*

Julian didn't wait for permission to improve the system. He took initiative. In that moment, he stopped being just an employee and started shaping the culture.

Why This Matters

In the previous stages, you learned to see the big picture (Awareness), align with the mission (Alignment), and use frameworks to solve problems (Application). But you can do all those things and still be passive. You can be a brilliant, aligned, framework-using waiter, standing ready for someone to order you into action.

Stage 4 is where you stop reacting and start generating.

Organizations die from stagnation. They calcify around old habits. They need **friction-hunters**. When employees wait for permission to think, the company moves at the speed of its slowest manager. When employees take initiative, the company moves at the speed of its collective intelligence and solves gaps before they become issues.

Core Concept & Framework: The Leverage Mindset

The Mindset Shift: **I don't wait for permission to think—I look for leverage.**

Initiative is not about doing *more* work—it is about finding *better* ways to work. It involves a specific set of behaviors that move you from a passenger to a driver:

- **Spotting Gaps:** Noticing where the current process fails or falls short.
- **Surfacing Friction:** Identifying the "pebbles in the shoe" that slow the team down.
- **Proposing Solutions:** Never bring a problem without a potential fix attached to it.

- **Asking Better Questions:** Shifting from "How do I do this?" to "Why do we do it this way?"
- **Influencing Teamwork:** Nudging peers toward better habits without needing formal authority.

The Impact of Frontline Strategic Thinking

Consider a family-owned plumbing business where the office manager became the catalyst for real change. While others focused on their assigned tasks, she went a step further, consistently noticing patterns in customer complaints and communication breakdowns that the spreadsheets didn't explain. She made a point of collecting client feedback directly, asking questions after calls and tracking the nature of inbound inquiries—especially those about appointment times, invoices, and payment options.

Instead of brushing off these concerns or reacting with piecemeal fixes, the office manager mapped out the entire customer journey. She asked "why" at every stage—why clients were calling repeatedly, why follow-ups were getting delayed, and why invoices weren't being accessed promptly. After identifying the gaps causing friction, she researched solutions and developed a plan to address them, including evaluating communication platforms and proposing one that provided real-time technician tracking, digital invoice access, and streamlined payment processing.

She presented a clear, data-backed proposal to the owners, outlining not only the customer benefits but also time and cost savings for the team. Working with both the admin and plumbing crews, she coordinated training sessions, created simple how-to guides, and piloted the new system with a small group of clients to measure results before a full rollout.

The outcomes were substantial—client call volume regarding appointment status dropped by half, repeat business from satisfied customers increased, and positive online reviews highlighted the ease of communication. Internally, less time was spent on status updates and administrative follow-ups, freeing up the team for higher-value work. The business saw growth in loyalty and a stronger reputation, all sparked by one office manager who looked beyond her daily checklist, spotted patterns and opportunities, and led a strategic shift. This example shows how ownership and intentional, strategic thinking from any seat in an organization can create lasting value and progress for the whole company.

Dual WIFM Lenses (What's In It For Me?)

Initiators take the next steps without being asked.

The Leader Lens

Why do you want a team of initiators? Because it creates scalability. You cannot be everywhere. You cannot see every broken process or unhappy customer. You need eyes and ears on the ground that are connected to brains that are empowered to act. When your team takes initiative, they clear the "noise" from your plate, allowing you to focus on the signal—the high-level strategic work that only you can do.

The Employee Lens

For you, initiative is the currency of credibility. The people who get promoted, who get the best projects, and who survive layoffs are rarely the ones who keep their heads down. They are the ones who advanced the work. Initiative builds your reputation as a "momentum generator." You become known as someone who not only identifies problems but also solves them.

Application: The "I Intend To" Experiment

How do we turn this desire for action into a daily habit?

For Leaders:

Create a "Safe-to-Fail" zone. If you punish every mistake, you kill initiative instantly. People will only take risks if they know they won't be executed for them.

- **The 24-Hour Rule:** When an employee brings you a problem, tell them, "Take 24 hours. Don't solve it yet. Come back tomorrow with three possible solutions and your recommendation."
- **Celebrate the Attempt:** Publicly praise someone who tried to fix a broken process, even if their solution wasn't perfect. Praise the *behavior* of initiative.

For Employees:

Avoid asking open-ended questions such as "What do you want me to do?" Start making statements.

- **The "Gap List":** Keep a notebook on your desk. Every time you feel frustration or see a wasted step, record it. Once a week, pick one item and ask, "What is the smallest thing I can do to fix this?"
- **The Proposal:** When you spot an opportunity, draft a one-page proposal. State the Problem, the Proposed Solution, and the Expected Benefit. Send it to your manager with the subject line: *"Idea to improve [Process Name]."*

Putting Ownership into Practice

Driving a culture of initiative begins with asking the right questions and encouraging action. Leaders can uncover hidden challenges by exploring friction points and actively supporting solutions, while employees can take ownership by proposing thoughtful changes to improve workflows. From rethinking unproductive meetings to piloting streamlined processes, these steps empower teams to address obstacles head-on and foster a proactive, solution-oriented environment.

Leader Action:

In your next team meeting, ask: *"Where is the friction? What is the one thing making your job harder than it needs to be?"* When they answer, ask the follow-up: *"What is one thing you could do this week to smooth that out? How can I support that action?"*

Employee Action:

Identify a recurring meeting that feels unproductive. Do not just complain about it. Send a note to the organizer (even if they are senior to you) saying: *"I've noticed we often rush the end of this meeting. I intend to prepare a 3-point summary of key data points beforehand so we can proceed directly to decisions. Would that be helpful?"*

Conversation Prompt:

"I noticed [Problem X] seems to be slowing us down. I've been thinking about a way to streamline it by doing [Solution Y]. I intend to pilot this in my next project to assess its effectiveness. Are there any red flags you see before I try?"

Transition

You have now moved from awareness to alignment, through application, and into initiative. You are spotting gaps and filling them. You are credible. You are effective. But true ownership is not just about fixing today's problems—it is about securing tomorrow's success.

STAGE 5: OWNERSHIP: LEAD, INSPIRE, AND CREATE CHANGE

"Inspiring leaders build confidence in others and help everyone see the value they bring to themselves and the organization." — Jamie Anne Gustafson

The Unofficial Leader

At a struggling software company, morale was at an all-time low after a series of layoffs. The official leaders were distant, locked in strategic meetings. The teams were anxious and directionless.

In the middle of this, an engineer named Maria started holding an optional "Lunch and Learn" every Friday. She wasn't a manager. She had no formal authority. Still, she saw that her colleagues were falling behind on new coding languages, so she decided to teach them what she knew.

The first session had three people. By the third, there were thirty. Maria didn't share code—she shared context. She connected the new languages back to the company's long-term product roadmap, which she had researched herself (Stage 1). She demonstrated that learning these skills would help them advance their careers and improve the company's products (Stage 2). She gave them simple frameworks for practicing (Stage 3). She took the initiative to start the whole thing without being asked (Stage 4).

Soon, other senior engineers volunteered to teach. The "Lunch and Learns" became a hub of innovation. People started prototyping new features. They started mentoring junior developers. Maria hadn't just taught a class. She reignited a culture. When a new Head of Engineering was hired, Maria was the first person they promoted to lead a team. But she had been leading all along.

Why This Matters

This final stage is the culmination of the journey. It's where ownership becomes a habit, not an action. You have moved through Awareness, Alignment, Application, and Initiative. You are no longer just a participant in the system—you are a force that shapes it.

This is the point where individuals become catalysts. A catalyst is a substance that accelerates a chemical reaction and lowers the activation energy. In an organization, a catalyst is a person whose thinking and behavior amplify the success of everyone around them.

They don't just solve problems; they create an environment in which issues are solved. They don't just innovate but inspire others to innovate. This is the ultimate expression of ownership because your focus shifts from your own contribution to your impact on the organization's capacity to win.

Core Concept & Framework: The Catalyst Mindset

The Mindset Shift: **My impact isn't just on the work—it's on the people, systems, and future of the organization.**

At this stage, you think like a leader, not a passenger. Your choices are filtered through a new set of questions. It's no longer "Is this the right decision for this project?" but "Is this decision good for the business? Will it help my team grow? Does it make us more resilient for the future?"

Ownership at this level manifests in specific, observable behaviors:

- **Modeling Resilience:** When a project fails, you are the first to talk about what was learned, not who was to blame.
- **Sharing Insights Generously:** You don't hoard knowledge to make yourself indispensable—you share it to make the team stronger.
- **Mentoring Others:** You actively look for opportunities to elevate the skills and confidence of your colleagues.
- **Strengthening Systems:** You don't just work within the system—you work *on* the system, making it better for the next person.
- **Championing Innovation:** You are a voice for the new, the better, the next—even when it's uncomfortable.

The Multiplier Effect

A Stage 5 owner is something different: they are a "10x leader," regardless of their title. They don't just produce ten times the output —they make ten other people more productive.

Think of it as the difference between being a star player and being the coach. The star player can win a game. The coach can build a dynasty.

When an employee reaches this level, they see themselves as stewards of the organization's health. They tell the organization's story forward, connecting the past with the future. They are the ones who onboard new hires, not just by showing them the coffee machine, but by explaining *why we do what we do here*. They are the ones who defend a risky but promising new idea in a meeting, giving it the air cover it needs to survive.

This is not about grand, heroic gestures. It's about the thousand small decisions you make when you start thinking like an owner. You stay late to help a junior colleague who is stuck, not because it's your job, but because their success is the team's success. You ask the quiet person in the room for their opinion because you know good ideas can come from anywhere. You become an amplifier.

Dual WIFM Lenses (What's In It For Me?)

The Leader Lens

Why cultivate catalysts? Because they are your succession plan. They are the future leaders of your organization, developing in plain sight. They make your job easier by distributing the burden of leadership. They are the immune system of your culture, protecting it from cynicism and mediocrity. When you have catalysts, your organization becomes self-healing and self-improving.

The Employee Lens

For you, this stage is about legacy. It's where you transition from building a career to building a reputation. You become known not just for what you do, but for the impact you have on others. This is the source of deep professional fulfillment. You aren't merely earning a paycheck. You are making a difference. Your influence extends far beyond your job description, and your work takes on a profound sense of purpose.

Application: From Impact to Amplification

How do we make this final, crucial leap?

For Leaders:

Your job is to get out of the way and give them a platform.

- **Delegate Authority, Not Just Tasks:** Give your catalysts ownership of a real problem, with a real budget and real decision-making power. Let them lead a new initiative or fix a broken department.
- **Shine a Spotlight:** When a Stage 5 owner mentors someone to success, celebrate both the mentor and the mentee. Publicly recognize the behaviors you want to see repeated. Make them a visible example of "what right looks like."

For Employees:

Your focus shifts from "me" to "we."

- **Find a Protégé:** Identify someone on your team who is stuck in Stage 1 or 2. Take them to coffee. Ask them about their goals. Find one thing you can teach them that will help them progress.
- **Fix a System:** Look for a process that isn't just inefficient but is actively causing burnout or frustration for others. Map out a better way and champion that change, even if it's not "your job."

Putting Ownership into Practice

Build the next generation!

Leader Action:

Identify the "Marias" in your organization. The unofficial leaders. The go-to problem solvers. Create a "Catalyst Council"—a small, informal group of these individuals from different departments. Meet with them once a month and ask one question: *"What is the single biggest opportunity we are missing as a company?"* Then listen.

Employee Action:

The next time you are in a meeting where a decision is being debated, stop thinking about which side you are on. Instead, ask: *"Which choice will make our organization stronger in a year?"* Frame your contribution around that long-term perspective.

Conversation Prompt:

"This is a great idea you've brought forward. Who on the team can you partner with to help you lead this change? How can we use this project to help them grow?"

Transition

The journey through the five stages is not a one-time trip. It is a loop. As you become a catalyst, you begin to guide others as they start their own journey at Stage 1. You have moved from being a student of ownership to becoming a teacher. You are no longer just designing your work—you are designing leaders.

8

WHY TRAINING FAILS WITHOUT FORMATION

"Empty words without daily intentionality and communication create false environments and missed opportunities." —Jamie Anne Gustafson

The company had invested heavily in a world-class leadership training program. For two full days, twenty high-potential managers were whisked away to an off-site retreat. They were immersed in workshops on strategic thinking, effective communication, and fostering innovation. They filled out checklists, role-played difficult conversations, and left with binders full of frameworks and a renewed sense of purpose.

On Monday morning, one of those managers, Jordan, returned to the office, ready to lead. He maintained a checklist for running more effective meetings. He tried to implement a new feedback model. But by 10 a.m., he was drowning in the same flood of urgent emails and back-to-back meetings that consumed him before the training. His team was too busy hitting their quarterly targets to entertain his new "strategic" questions. His own boss, when asked about creating space for innovation, said, "Great idea, Jordan. Just don't let it distract you from the numbers."

Within two weeks, the binder was gathering dust on his shelf. The checklists were forgotten. Nothing had changed. The training event was a success, but the leadership transformation was a failure.

WHY THIS MATTERS

This story is the quiet reality in most organizations. We invest in training "events", workshops, seminars, and off-sites, hoping to install new skills, but we fail to build the environment where those skills can take root. Why does this matter? Without a supportive structure, even the best training is only a momentary spark of motivation. It doesn't forge new behaviors. It creates a temporary high, followed by a frustrating crash when employees return to a system that rewards the old way of doing things. You end up with inspired employees in a system that demands compliance, a recipe for cynicism and wasted investment.

CORE CONCEPT & FRAMEWORK

The core concept of this chapter is simple: **Training provides information—formation builds identity.**

Training is an event. It gives you a checklist, a tool, or a concept. Formation is a process. It's the structured, supported practice of using that tool until it becomes a natural behavior. Checklists don't create leaders because leadership isn't a task to be completed—it's a way of thinking to be cultivated.

Consider this: We can inundate people with information, but change occurs only when that information is lived out through practice, feedback, and accountability over time. The real work—the day-in, day-out execution—requires a different kind of support. It requires a system of formation.

BEYOND TRAINING: BUILDING LEADERS THROUGH THE PROCESS OF FORMATION

When Chris's small business first started, it was a close-knit team of passionate individuals, all working tirelessly to keep things running. Everyone was skilled at their jobs and dedicated to the company's success. But as the business grew, challenges began to emerge. While tasks were being completed, the team struggled to think beyond the immediate. They were reactive rather than proactive, solving problems in the moment but rarely stepping back to ask, "How can we make this better?

Chris recognized the issue. She had built the business from the ground up and was proud of how far they'd come, but she knew they couldn't sustain growth with their current approach. Chris wanted her team to take ownership, think strategically, and feel empowered to make decisions. She realized that this required more than just knowledge—it required a shift in mindset and behavior.

Initially, Chris tried a quick fix. She brought in a consultant to run a one-day workshop on leadership and problem-solving. The team left the session feeling inspired, full of ideas, and motivated. But within a week, the lessons faded. The daily grind took over, and the team reverted to their old habits. Chris realized that a single burst of training wasn't enough to create lasting change.

Determined to find a better solution, Chris introduced a new approach—structured, ongoing practice. She implemented weekly team challenges designed to help employees apply specific concepts to their work. Each week, the team focused on a single idea, such as identifying bottlenecks, improving communication, or enhancing the customer experience. They were encouraged to experiment, reflect on their experiences, and share their findings with the group.

At first, the team was hesitant. They were used to following instructions, not stepping outside their comfort zones. Chris reassured them that this wasn't about getting it perfect—it was about learning and growing. She encouraged them to take risks, make mistakes, and view failures as opportunities to improve.

One of the first challenges focused on identifying inefficiencies. Ken, who managed inventory, noticed that their tracking system was outdated and prone to errors. Instead of simply flagging the issue, he researched potential solutions and proposed a new system to the team. With Chris's support, they implemented the change, which saved time and reduced mistakes. Ken's initiative inspired others to start looking for inefficiencies in their own areas.

The weekly challenges became a cornerstone of the team's development. Chris facilitated discussions where employees shared their successes, struggles, and lessons learned. She asked thoughtful questions to help them reflect: "What made this approach work?" "What would you do differently next time?" "How does this connect to our larger goals?" These conversations reinforced the importance of learning through action and created a culture of continuous improvement.

Over time, the team began to shift. They stopped waiting for Chris to solve problems and started solving them on their own. They didn't just complete tasks, they looked for ways to improve them. They didn't fear failure—they saw it as a stepping stone to growth. And they didn't just focus on their individual roles—they started to see how their work contributed to the business's success.

One of the most significant changes came when the team tackled a recurring issue with delayed shipments. Instead of accepting it as an unavoidable problem, they worked together to find a solution. They streamlined their packing process, improved communication with customers, and negotiated better terms with their shipping provider. The result? Faster deliveries, happier customers, and a team that felt proud of their collective achievement.

Chris's approach exemplified the principles of formation. She didn't just provide her team with information—she created an environment where they could practice, reflect, and grow. The structured challenges, combined with cycles of feedback and support, helped her team develop the habits and mindset of strategic thinkers. They became proactive problem-solvers who could navigate complexity, adapt to change, and drive meaningful results.

The transformation wasn't immediate, but it was profound. Chris's team grew from a group of task-doers to a team of leaders, each taking ownership of their work and contributing to the business's success. The process of formation—structured practice, honest feedback, and intentional growth—didn't just improve the team's performance. It created a culture of curiosity, collaboration, and continuous improvement that became the foundation of the business's success.

DUAL WIFM LENSES (WHAT'S IN IT FOR ME?)

Leader Lens: Why This Matters Upstream

Shifting your perspective from being a buyer of training events to an architect of developmental systems transforms how you approach growth. Instead of asking, "Who should attend this workshop?", you start by asking, "How can we foster an environment for continuous growth?" This mindset safeguards your investment by ensuring that the skills acquired through training evolve into lasting habits rather than fading into forgotten ideas. By building a repeatable, reinforcing process, you eliminate the need to start from scratch with each new hire. Instead, you create a culture that consistently develops leaders and owners, driving sustainable growth and long-term success.

Employee Lens: Why This Matters on the Ground

Having structure provides the foundation to build habits and confidence, turning intentions into sustained practice with the support needed along the way. It's the difference between making a resolution and actually sticking to it. In a culture that values trial, reflection, and learning, perfection isn't expected on the first try. Instead, experimentation and growth are encouraged, creating an environment where real progress is possible. Beyond mere inspiration, this approach helps you develop tangible skills and witness the direct impact of your actions—building credibility and genuine influence in your role.

APPLICATION: TURNING INSIGHT INTO PRACTICE

The lesson is that company culture shapes outcomes far more than a new tool or event ever could. To make true progress, stop seeking quick-fix training events and start laying the foundation for habitual reinforcement. Develop a regular rhythm for practice, feedback, and reflection within your team.

Leaders should see their responsibility as shaping the environment, not just enforcing milestones. That means integrating cycles of practice and honest feedback into everyday work. For employees, taking the initiative to learn and reflect with peers or mentors goes much further than waiting for the next workshop.

PUTTING OWNERSHIP INTO PRACTICE

Building new habits takes intentional effort and collaboration.

Leader Action:

Choose one concept, like reviewing a team process or mapping a recent challenge, and lead a 30-minute team practice session focused on real, pressing work. Treat this as a chance to develop skills and provide feedback, not just to complete a checklist. Build in time to solicit employees' perspectives and feedback. Use a framework to ensure shared language.

Employee Action:

Pair up with a colleague to hold each other accountable for trying out a new behavior or approach. Check in weekly, share what you tried, and discuss what you learned. Focus on the process, not perfection. Teach each other tips and tricks. Set up a "lifeline" channel on your direct messenger to reach out when you need someone to help keep the needle moving.

Conversation Prompt:

"We've all discussed new ways of working—what's one practice we can try together this month so it moves from idea to habit?"

READY FOR THE NEXT STEP?

The journey to intentional leadership doesn't end here—it begins with action. While this book provides the frameworks and insights to transform contributors into catalysts. The real impact, however, comes from putting these principles into practice.

I've guided countless individuals and teams through the 5 Stages of Ownership, helping them integrate these concepts into their organizations to drive innovation, foster connection, and create a culture of leadership at every level. Now, I'm here to help you do the same.

Your next step is to bring these ideas to life within your team. Book Jamie Anne Gustafson, PhD, to teach these valuable insights and guide your organization in developing the "how " of your specific leadership formation. Together, we'll create a system that turns potential into performance and builds leaders who inspire, empower, and transform.

Let's take this journey together.

FROM FIRST DAY
TO FUTURE LEADER
INTEGRATING OWNERSHIP
INTO ONBOARDING AND
SUCCESSION PLANNING

Most organizations treat onboarding and succession planning as separate functions, managed at opposite ends of an employee's lifecycle. Onboarding is a flurry of paperwork, system logins, and initial training designed to get a new hire productive as quickly as possible. Succession planning, on the other hand, is often a high-level, infrequent conversation about who might eventually fill the top boxes on the organizational chart.

What if these two processes were not separate but two points on a single, continuous path? What if your onboarding process was the first step in identifying and developing your next generation of leaders? This is the power of integrating the 5 Stages of Ownership into the very fabric of your talent strategy. By doing so, you create a seamless journey that guides an employee from their first day (Awareness) to their future leadership role (Ownership).

This chapter will show you how to connect the 5 Stages of Ownership to your onboarding and succession planning, creating a powerful system for intentional leadership development.

ONBOARDING: THE FIRST STEP ON THE OWNERSHIP JOURNEY

Traditional onboarding answers the question, "What do I need to do?" An ownership-focused approach answers a more powerful question: "How does my work help us win?" This shift in perspective transforms onboarding from a procedural checklist into the first stage of leadership formation.

Let's look at how the first few stages of ownership can be woven into your onboarding process.

Stage 1: Awareness: Seeing the Bigger Picture from Day One

The goal here is to move a new employee from passive recipient to active participant. Instead of showing them their desk and their task list, you invite them into the organization's ecosystem.

- **Traditional Onboarding:** "Here are the company values. Sign this form saying you've read them."
- **Ownership Onboarding:** "We want you to spend an hour each day identifying what our customers value about this company. Then highlight how you believe we create that value intentionally."

Practical Strategies:

- **The "Company Safari":** Task new hires with scheduling short, 15-minute introductory meetings with people from different departments. Their goal isn't to learn how to do their job, but to ask, "What does your team do, and how does it connect to what my team does?"

- **Strategic Document Access:** Grant new hires access to the company's strategic plan or quarterly goals. This sends a clear message: "We trust you, and we want you to think like an owner from the start."

Benefit: New employees quickly grasp how their role fits into the larger mission, accelerating engagement and a sense of purpose. They begin their tenure feeling valued as a member of the team, not just a cog in the machine.

Stage 2: Alignment: Connecting Role to Mission

Once a new hire understands the bigger picture, the next step is helping them find their place within it. Alignment is about connecting their personal strengths and goals with the company's needs and vision.

- **Traditional Onboarding:** "This is your job description. These are your KPIs."
- **Ownership Onboarding:** "Let's look at your job description together. Where do you see your greatest strengths aligning with these responsibilities? What part of this role excites you most, and how can we help you lean into that?"

Practical Strategies:

- **Strengths-Based Check-in:** In the first 60 days, have managers sit down with new employees to discuss their inherent strengths (using tools like CliftonStrengths or simply through conversation). The focus is on leveraging those strengths to meet and exceed job expectations.

- **Goal-Setting Collaboration:** Instead of handing down goals, co-create them. Ask the new employee, "Based on what you know about our team's objectives, what goals do you think you could set for yourself in the next 90 days?"

Benefit: This approach fosters personal investment. When employees see a clear link between their daily effort, their personal strengths, and the company's vision, their motivation shifts from extrinsic (a paycheck) to intrinsic (a sense of purpose and contribution).

SUCCESSION PLANNING: IDENTIFYING LEADERS ON THE JOURNEY

Succession planning is often viewed as a risky bet on "high-potential" individuals. But when you use the 5 Stages of Ownership as a guide, it becomes a process of observation and development. The journey itself reveals who is ready—and willing—to lead.

As employees move beyond the initial stages of Awareness and Alignment, they begin to demonstrate behaviors that clearly indicate leadership aptitude.

Stage 3: Application: The Proving Ground

Application is where employees start using frameworks to create value. They move from knowing *what* to do to understanding *how* to think about their work. This is where you can start to see who has the potential to solve problems, not just complete tasks.

Identifying Future Leaders:

- Look for the employee who doesn't just use a tool you gave them, but adapts it for a new situation.
- Notice the team member who, after learning about the company's SWOT analysis, brings you a thoughtful observation about how a strength can overcome a potential threat or weakness.
- These individuals are demonstrating the ability to think strategically and apply concepts to create value.

Stage 4: Initiative: From Passenger to Driver

This is a critical turning point. Employees at this stage stop waiting for permission to think. They identify gaps, propose solutions, and seek ways to improve the system without being asked.

Identifying Future Leaders:

- The employee who says, "I noticed our client intake process has a lot of friction. I have an idea for how we could streamline it," is showing initiative.
- The team member who organizes a quick huddle to solve a cross-functional problem before it escalates is acting like a leader, regardless of their title.
- These are the people who see problems as opportunities. They are your emerging leaders.

Stage 5: Ownership: The Catalyst for Change

At this final stage, ownership is a habit. These individuals think like leaders naturally. Their focus is on the impact of decisions on people, systems, and the organization's future. They don't just amplify their own success—they amplify the success of everyone around them.

Identifying Future Leaders:

These are your succession candidates. They are the ones mentoring others without being asked, asking questions about the business's long-term health, and taking responsibility for both team failures and successes. They have proven their readiness to lead through their actions.

THE INTEGRATED SYSTEM: A VIRTUOUS CYCLE

When you connect onboarding and succession planning through the 5 Stages of Ownership, you create a powerful, self-reinforcing system.

- **Onboarding sets the stage for leadership.** By introducing Awareness and Alignment from day one, you establish a culture where thinking like an owner is the standard, not the exception.
- **The journey reveals true leadership potential.** Instead of guessing who might be a good leader, you can observe who demonstrates the behaviors of Application, Initiative, and Ownership over time.
- **Succession becomes a matter of recognition, not selection.** Your future leaders are defined by their progression along the ownership path. Your job is simply to recognize their growth and provide them with the opportunities to continue it.

- **Leaders who have completed the journey become the best teachers.** They naturally mentor new employees through the stages because they have walked the same path themselves, creating a virtuous cycle of leadership development.

Adopting this integrated approach means you stop leaving leadership to chance. You design a system that intentionally cultivates it from an employee's first day to their last, ensuring your organization has a robust pipeline of leaders ready to guide it into the future.

INTEGRATING INSIGHT
A GUIDE FOR READING AND
DISCUSSING TOGETHER

Reading a book is often a solitary act. We curl up in a chair, highlight a few passages, and perhaps nod in agreement with a new idea. However, leadership formation is a communal sport. It doesn't happen in isolation. It happens in the messy, dynamic interactions between people. To truly transform your organization, you need to take these concepts off the page and into the room where work actually happens.

This chapter is designed to help you do just that. Whether you are an HR professional looking to reshape culture, an executive guiding a vision, or a manager trying to get your team to step up, this guide will help you turn this book into a tool for shared learning and collective action.

The goal isn't to finish the book. The goal is to build a shared language. When everyone on the team understands what "moving from Awareness to Alignment" means, you stop wasting time explaining *why* change is needed and start focusing on *how* to execute it.

TAILORING THE APPROACH BY ROLE

Different roles will look through different lenses. Here is how to approach the text based on your role in the organization.

For HR Professionals: The Architects

You are reading this book to audit your systems. As you move through the chapters, ask yourself if your current structures support or stifle ownership.

- **Focus:** Pay close attention to the chapters on the 5 Stages of Ownership. Do your job descriptions reflect these stages? Does your performance review process reward "Initiative" or just compliance?
- **Action:** Use the book to facilitate a "Culture Audit" with your leadership team. Identify where your current policies may inadvertently create passive employees rather than active owners.

For Senior Leaders: The Visionaries

You are reading this book to signal importance. If you don't value this journey, no one else will. Your role is to connect the "Four S's" (Strategy, Synergy, Systems, Stories) to the company's long-term vision.

- **Focus:** Zero in on the strategic elements. How does the "Accidental Leader" problem threaten your succession pipeline?
- **Action:** Don't just assign the reading—participate in the discussion. Share your own stories of when you were stuck in the "Awareness" stage and how you learned to take ownership. Vulnerability from the top enables growth at the bottom.

For Managers: The Builders

You are reading this book to solve immediate friction. You need tactical tools to help your team execute better today.

- **Focus:** Lean heavily into the practical frameworks. The transition from "Application" to "Initiative" is likely where your biggest headaches and biggest opportunities live.
- **Action:** Use the book as a coaching manual. When a direct report comes to you with a problem, use the language of the book to guide them. Ask, "Are we stuck in Awareness here, or do we need to move to Application?"

FORMATS FOR DISCUSSION

Trying to tackle the whole book in one sitting often leads to information overload. Instead, choose a format that fits your team's rhythm.

The "Slow Roll" (Weekly Stand-ups)

Perfect for busy operational teams who can't spare an hour for a book club.

- **Structure:** Dedicate the first 15 minutes of your weekly team meeting to one concept.
- **Process:** Assign one short section (e.g., "Stage 1: Awareness") to a different team member each week. Their job is to summarize it in two minutes and pose one question to the group.
- **Benefit:** Keeps the concepts top-of-mind without overwhelming the schedule.

The "Deep Dive" Workshop (Monthly)

Best for leadership teams or cross-functional groups.

- **Structure:** A 60-to-90-minute session focused on a major theme (e.g., "The 5 Stages" or "The Four S's").
- **Process:** Ask everyone to read the relevant chapters beforehand. Spend the first 10 minutes refreshing the core concepts, then spend the rest of the time workshopping a real business problem using those concepts.
- **Benefit:** Moves directly from theory to practice. You aren't talking *about* the book but using it to do work.

The Cross-Functional Book Club

Ideal for breaking down silos and building a cross-departmental culture.

- **Structure:** A voluntary lunch-and-learn series open to anyone in the organization.
- **Process:** Mix groups so that sales, operations, and IT are sitting at the same table. Discuss how "Synergy" (one of the Four S's) looks different in each department.
- **Benefit:** Creates empathy and understanding across the organization, which is essential for the "Alignment" stage.

THE FACILITATOR'S GUIDE: QUESTIONS TO SPARK INSIGHT

Great discussions don't happen by accident—they happen through great questions. Avoid yes/no questions like "Did you like the chapter?" Instead, use these prompts to dig deeper.

General Reflection

- "Which of the 5 Stages do you think our team spends the most time in? Why?"
- "Was there a moment in the book where you felt called out? What was the uncomfortable truth you recognized?"
- "If we fully embraced the concept of 'Ownership' as described here, what is one thing we would stop doing immediately?"

Stage-Specific Questions

- **Awareness:** "What is one piece of information you wish you had sooner that would have helped you see the bigger picture?"
- **Alignment:** "Do you feel your personal strengths are currently aligned with the company's mission? If not, where is the gap?"
- **Application:** "Where do we have a 'knowing-doing gap?' Where do we know the right thing to do but fail to execute it?"
- **Initiative:** "What is a friction point in our daily work that everyone ignores? How could we apply initiative to fix it?"

Action-Oriented Questions

- "Who is someone on another team you need to build better Synergy with this week?"
- "What is one system we have that is currently preventing ownership?"
- "How will we hold each other accountable to these standards next week?"

MOVING FROM TALK TO ACTION

The danger of book discussions is that they can become "intellectual tourism"—we visit the ideas, take some photos, and then go back home to our old habits. To prevent this, end every discussion with a commitment.

The "One Thing" Rule

At the end of your session, go around the room. Each person must state one specific change they will make before the next meeting, based on what they read. It could be as simple as "I will ask, 'How does this help us win?' before starting my next project."

Accountability Partners

Pair people up. Their job is to check in once a week for five minutes to ask, "How are you doing with your commitment?" This peer-to-peer accountability is often more powerful than manager oversight.

Pilot Projects

If a discussion reveals a major flaw in your systems (like a broken onboarding process or a communication silo), don't just complain about it. Create a small task force to apply the book's frameworks to fix it. Treat it as a pilot project for the "Initiative" stage.

Reading this book together signals that you are ready to grow. It says that you are not satisfied with accidental leadership—you are ready to design your future on purpose. So, open the pages, start the conversation, and let the transformation begin.

ABOUT ME

I am a strategic management consultant, educator, C-suite leader, and thought leader with a passion for cultivating leadership at every level. My journey has been shaped through a diverse background— serving in the military, leading community initiatives, and guiding businesses through ownership journeys and succession planning. With a PhD in Strategic Management and years of experience as a professor, consultant, and executive, I've dedicated my career to bridging the gap between vision and execution.

Leadership is not accidental; it's intentional. It is forged through experience, strategic thinking, and a commitment to growth. This philosophy led to the creation of the 5-Stage Ownership Journey, a transformative framework that empowers individuals to move from awareness to true ownership. Personal strengths are aligned with organizational goals to help businesses unlock their potential and foster cultures where leadership emerges organically.

My approach combines academic rigor with practical application. Whether guiding executives, mentoring rising leaders, or helping teams navigate challenges, I provide the tools, language, and confidence needed to inspire meaningful change. Leadership, to me, is about creating space for others to thrive, innovate, and contribute to sustainable success.

HOW I CAN HELP YOU

- **Strategic Leadership:** I help bridge the gap between vision and execution, ensuring your goals are met with precision and care.
- **Team Empowerment:** I mentor teams to be motivated, collaborative, and impactful.
- **Community Development:** I create initiatives that strengthen communities and foster growth.
- **Problem-Solving Expertise:** I bring innovative and practical solutions to tackle challenges and drive results.

ACHIEVEMENTS & HONORS

- **Education:** PhD in Strategic Management, Master's in Organizational Management, and a Bachelor's in Business Administration.

- **Awards:** Agent of the Year (2013), Air Force Commendation Medal (2010), and more.
- **Military Service:** Honored with the Iraqi Campaign Medal and Air Force Expeditionary Service Ribbon.

Leadership is a journey, not a destination. It is about showing up prepared, resilient, and rooted in purpose. Let's connect and explore how we can work together to create lasting impact for your business or community.

Connect with me at jamiegustafson.com or

Email me at info@jamiegustafson.com to start the conversation.

www.ingramcontent.com/pod-product-compliance
Lightning Source LLC
Chambersburg PA
CBHW060207070426
42447CB00035B/2821